Graduate Admissions Essays

What Works, What Doesn't, and Why

Donald Asher

TEN SPEED PRESS
Berkeley, California

Ten Speed Press
Box 7123
Berkeley, CA 94707

Library of Congress Cataloging-in-Publication Data

Asher, Donald.
    Graduate admissions essays: what works, what doesn't, and why / Donald Asher.
      p.   cm.
    ISBN 0-89815-414-6
    1. Universities and colleges—United States—Graduate work—Entrance examinations.
2. Universities and colleges—United States—Graduate work—Admissions. 3. Exposition
(Rhetoric) 4. Essay—Examinations—Study guides. I. Title.
LB2366.2.A84   1991
378.1'057—dc20   90-29019 CIP

First Printing, 1991

Printed in the United States of America

   7 8 9 10 — 99 98 97 96

To your success

■ ACKNOWLEDGEMENTS ■

I owe special thanks to Ms. Maureen Daly, Mr. Kilian Kerwin and Ms. Catherine Glew, who opened their Rolodexes to me early in the progress of this book, and to their friends who introduced me to their friends who introduced me to their friends. May we all have so many and such caliber of friends and acquaintances. Many special thanks to the contributors: Mr. Todd Hobler, Mr. Adam N. Green, Ms. Flay Rogers, Ms. Ruby Ausbrooks, Ms. Maureen Daly, Ms. Margie Lariviere, Ms. Andrea J. Morgan, Mr. Brad Wurtz, Mr. Meyer M. Speary, Ms. H. Glickman, Mr. Bob Muldoon, Mr. Victor F. Simonyi, Mr. Kevin Kelleher, Ms. Gennine Zinner, Mr. R. D., Ms. Jennifer Ferenstein, Ms. Lisa Kemmerer, Ms. Linda C. Saremi, Ms. Gretchen Craft, Ms. Wendy Richardson, Mr. Tod Cochran, Ms. Molly Stenzel, Ms. Deborah E. Gallant, Mr. Brian Boyl, Ms. Sabrina Gee, Ms. Anastasia Pinoris, Mr. David Lawrence Conlin, Mr. David Coleman, Dr. Bruce Johnson, Mr. Kevan Shokat, Dr. John R. Vásquez, Ms. Debbie Redd, Mr. Shane Whittington, Ms. Rebecca Weller, Dr. Majid Tavakkolijou, and of course, anonymous.

Many of the names, dates, schools, firm names, and other specific details in these essays were changed at the request of the contributors, and others were changed at the discretion of the editors. No particular individual named in these essays should be presumed to be any particular actual individual, and any such assumption would be unwarranted.

Special thanks to Mr. Samuel T. Lindquist, Director of Admissions, The Amos Tuck School of Business Administration; Dr. Gerald Foster, Director of Admissions, Harvard Medical School; Mr. Richard Badger, Dean of Admissions, The Law School of the University of Chicago; Ms. Kathleen Plessas, Director of Admissions, School of Medicine, University of California, San Francisco; Ms. Judy Colwell, Assistant Director of Admissions, Stanford University School of Medicine; Dr. Barbara A. Herman, University of Wisconsin—Madison Medical School; Dr. Thomas Q. Reefe, Director, Career Services Center, University of California, Santa Cruz; Mr. Peter S. Van Houten and Ms. Mary Blakeslee, Pre-Professional/Pre-Graduate Advising, University of California, Berkeley; Dr. Dandré Desandies, Undergraduate Advising Center, Stanford University; Ms. Toinette Menashe, Director, Master of Arts in Liberal Studies Program, Reed College; Prof. Walter Englert, Classics, Reed College; Ms. Patty Cassidy, Director, Career Planning & Placement Office, Reed College; Ms. Lisa Garb, Director of Public Relations, Peterson's Guides; and the many admissions directors, counselors, and staff who spoke with me quite frankly but who did not wish to be mentioned by name.

Many thanks to Ms. Kathleen Docherty, as always, this time for running my business while I researched and wrote this book. Many special thanks to Ms. Mariah Bear and Ms. Becky Lemov for copyediting the manuscript with their usual care. Special thanks as always to Phil, George, Sal, and Maureen. The errors are all mine, but many, many people have contributed to the success of this book. Thank you all.

■ TABLE OF CONTENTS ■

HOW TO USE THIS BOOK

The best way to use this book is to read it in its entirety, even the sections that do not apply to you directly. Then start over, completing each assignment before you go on to the next. Plan on rewriting your essay several times. Whatever you do, do not write a word until you have done the personal assessments in Chapter 3, *Self-Assessments: Getting Ready to Write.*

If you have procrastinated until the last minute the first thing you need to do is—*relax.* You can still finish a great essay by tomorrow morning. Just take out a pad of paper and a pen, read this book in order, follow its suggestions and do the assignments as you come across them. Do not read ahead, and just skip any sections that do not apply to your particular case.

This book makes several assumptions about you, the reader. Readers tend to be much smarter than average humans, and given this book's topic, it is probably safe to assume that you are much smarter than the average reader. It is a luxury to write for such an audience. Incidentally, after years of having college professors focus on your errors and shortcomings, you are probably a lot smarter than you think.

This book is designed to get you into the graduate program of your choice. *Your* choice. So the second assumption about you, the reader, is that you know what subject matter you wish to pursue. Chapter 1, *Choosing a School or Program,* gives some excellent tips and some warnings on investigating particular graduate programs, but the choice of subject matter must originate with you. If you are not sure whether you want to be a lawyer or a mathematician, you will need to seek counsel elsewhere before beginning your application process. Your parents, your parents' friends, your friends' parents, your school's faculty, preprofessional advising office, and/or office of career planning can all help you get a good start on your career goals decision-making process. Above all else, however, you must find some lawyers and some mathematicians and really talk to them.

If you bought this book or someone bought it for you because you are just thinking about going to graduate school, here is some free advice: *Go for it.* Society needs your advanced skills and, on purely personal grounds, education enriches life like no other experience or possession. Many of the top programs pay *you* to attend, except for the preprofessional schools, where you pay now and earn later (or borrow now and pay later). Besides, whether you are 21 or 80, you will never be younger than you are today, and there will never be a better time to continue your studies than right now.

One of the unique features of this book is its inclusion of a full chapter on letters of recommendation (Chapter 7). Letters of recommendation are a critical component of your application process, and they deserve full and separate consideration. In addition to providing a plan for selecting and motivating authors of letters of recommendation, this chapter gives you valuable advice on how to actually write your own. This will be useful in dealing with those professors who skirt their obligations by saying, "You draft it up and I'll sign it." As lamentable as this may be, it is common even at the best universities. If you are a good writer it is anything but lamentable—it is a golden opportunity, but not one which everybody would choose to have foisted upon her.

Another unique feature is the inclusion of scholarship, residency, fellowship, postgraduate, and postdoctoral essays. This information was available in no other book at the time this edition went to press. Essays become more precise, more specific, and less personal in a seamless continuum as one proceeds up the ivory tower. Reading these samples will help you see your own project in the larger context of academic essay and proposal writing, even if it is somewhat more basic.

This book's goal is to take all the mystery and most of the stress out of the graduate applications process, and guide the reader through drafting a compelling graduate admissions essay. This is also a resource book, as supplementary reading and other materials are recommended in the text where appropriate. The information on financial aid, graduate admissions testing, and other aspects of the graduate admissions process are included to give a clearer picture of the graduate essay as an integral part of the entire application process. This book is not intended to replace the advice of professors, college career counselors, and undergraduate advising officers.

While you cannot change who you are and what you have done with your life so far, you *can* make a good graduate application. Students tend to under- rather than overestimate their academic value. The number of students fully qualified for graduate study far exceeds the number who actually apply. To the extent that this book facilitates your application and contributes to the realization of your potential, so shall it be judged.

■ CHAPTER 1 ■

CHOOSING A SCHOOL OR PROGRAM

The biggest mistake you can make in selecting a graduate program is to blindly choose "the best program I can get into." Annual magazine rankings notwithstanding, there is no one criterion, no single hierarchy of good-better-best on which to base such a decision. You must consider several criteria and develop your own standards for evaluation.

If your choice is good, there will be a good fit between you and the program; you will enjoy your studies, you will find friends among faculty and fellow students, and your education will further your career goals both directly and indirectly. If your choice is poor, just imagine the opposite.

This chapter will guide you through the process of compiling and ranking a list of the good-better-best programs *for you,* and the following chapters will tell you how to get in.

Your first step is to poll all your personal contacts for recommendations of good graduate programs in your area of interest. There is no substitute for this person-to-person fact-finding mission, no written or databased resource that can replace the nuances of conversation. You should contact professors at your undergraduate school who would know about developments in your chosen field. Do not worry about

Reprinted from BIG IDEAS © 1983 Lynda Barry, with permission of the Real Comet Press.

whether you have ever taken a class from them; just call them up and introduce yourself. You should seek out former colleagues who are currently graduate students at targeted schools, and be sure to get recommendations from people who are currently employed in your future profession.

1

This survey will generate a core list of viable schools. To round out this preliminary list, visit the undergraduate advising center at your college or university (some schools combine undergraduate advising services with their office of career planning and placement). This office will vary from institution to institution, but the best are resource centers jammed full of guides, program catalogs, and scholarship and financial aid information, as well as talented, overworked counselors who can help you select a program, plan your application, and edit and polish your graduate essay.

The *Peterson's Guides* to graduate study are but one example of the type of resource a good undergraduate advising center will have for you. These annual guides are:

Peterson's Guide to Graduate & Professional Programs: An Overview

Peterson's Guide to Graduate Programs in Business, Education, Health, and Law

Peterson's Guide to Graduate Programs in the Humanities and Social Sciences

Peterson's Guide to Graduate Programs in the Physical Sciences and Mathematics

Peterson's Guide to Graduate Programs in the Biological and Agricultural Sciences

Peterson's Guide to Graduate Programs in Engineering and Applied Sciences

Peterson's Guides are particularly useful because they list each program's phone number, as well as the name of the program's dean, chair, or director. You will need the phone number, because as soon as you have an interest in a program, you should call and ask for a catalog. With some regrettable exceptions, catalogs are free, although they may take several agonizing weeks to arrive.

There are hundreds of other specialized guides for programs in fine arts, geography, marine sciences, film, environmental engineering, dance, teaching English as a second or foreign language, religion, business, women's studies, and so on, ad infinitum. Some of these guides are listed in the bibliography to this book.

If your undergraduate advising center is nonexistent or parochial, then, unfortunately, the full burden of research falls upon you. *Peterson's Guides* can be found in almost all major libraries, but the hundreds of other, lesser-known guides may not be. A few trips to local libraries and good bookstores are definitely in order, but remember that word of mouth is still the best first step. Be creative. You might call or write the French Embassy in Washington D.C. and ask which, in their opinion, are the best French language programs in this country. You might look in the *Encyclopedia of Associations*, discover that there is an American Speech-Language Hearing Association, call them (their number is provided right there in the encyclopedia), and discover that they publish a *Guide to Graduate Education in Speech-Language Pathology & Audiology*.

At first, concentrate on compiling a list of viable programs. Do not worry about ranking them in any firm order yet, just get as much information as you can. Once you have your list, you will be able to pursue the ranking and selection process.

The process of selecting a graduate program involves balancing at least four main components: the academics, the people, the locale, and the cost.

The academics can be thought of as the intellectual feast. What are you going to learn? Hopefully, it will be something you want to learn. Read the journals in your field. Where do the people who are writing material you find exciting teach? Ask your professors to evaluate the schools on your list, then ask for suggestions of *particular professors, writers, and researchers* who could further your academic interests. Professors are your number one source of really useful information about graduate programs—talk to them often.

If you are evaluating preprofessional schools—business, law, medicine, architecture, and so on—it is somewhat more difficult to discern the difference between programs. Nevertheless, these schools are each quite distinct, and understanding this not only increases your chances of finding the right one for you, it also increases your chances of developing a compelling application and gaining admission to your first-choice schools.

For example, some medical schools have an emphasis on public health built into the regular medical school curriculum, others offer a special combined M.D./M.P.H. program, some have both. Some teaching medical centers are located in the heart of decayed urban centers, taking pride in serving disadvantaged patient populations, while others are famous for their cardiology units, or their pediatric hospitals. Some architecture schools are known worldwide for their concern with handicapped access and other social issues, while others are known as slavish devotees to design in the International Style of Mies van der Rohe. Failing to research such differences between programs is about as careless as going to the lake and diving headfirst into unknown waters. Obviously, if you are applying to thirty medical schools you cannot take a year off and research every one of them, but you should have a very well defined impression of your top three to five choices.

Be careful of confusing reputation with academics. A school's reputation is certainly a consideration, but what you are going to learn is far more important. If reputation is highly important to you, you need to evaluate it carefully. Since reputations lag behind current conditions by three to five years, a school's current reputation may reflect circumstances that have passed. A school's reputation in five to ten years will be more important to your career than its reputation at the moment you matriculate. So you should analyze and project long-term trends, and not fixate on any one year's rankings. My personal recommendation is to ignore reputation and concentrate on what the program can offer you. Learning nothing of use to you and being miserable at the Number One School of Business is probably not as good for your career as being really excited about the entrepreneurial program at the Number Thirty School of Business. Think about it.

Read the catalogs from graduate programs *carefully*. Although they may all seem to have been written by the same public relations firm in St. Louis, there are always subtle tip-offs to the atmosphere and special emphases of each particular school. Besides, the catalogs usually have profiles of faculty, and that brings us to our next point: People.

All other things being equal, people are the most important component of your graduate education. This means the faculty and fellow students with whom you will live and work closely for the next two to six years, or more. You want to be sure that you can work with them, and that they can work with you. If you went to a large university, you may not have spent more than twenty hours in your entire undergraduate career in the presence of a full professor, but you are about to work hand in glove with them, on research that they will monitor closely. If the best place in the world to study fractals is a program dominated by tyrannical gargoyles, you might want to take a look at the other schools on your list.

Similarly, if you have just spent four years fighting every day for the creation of a major in feminist political theory, do yourself a favor and follow your mentors. Graduate school is not a good place to pioneer a new program focus or to study without guidance. Although forging a new path is not impossible, studying in a program that aligns with your interests will probably be more gratifying and productive. When you choose a school whose program closely matches your interests *and* your application essay explains this clearly, that essay can vault you farther than your grades and test scores ever could.

Now for a major warning against choosing a graduate program because of one or more professors: Professors move, go on sabbatical, die, and change their beliefs! If a specific professor is of great interest to you, write her to be sure that she is going to stay, and begin to establish intellectual rapport. Such contact can be the foundation for a successful application.

The school's physical locale will be important to some applicants, and totally irrelevant to others. If you are committed to your studies, you will not be too concerned with the weather or the proximity of ocean beaches. However, if you truly believe that you will be miserable in New York city, or Iowa City for that matter, then that has to be a factor in your decision. Wherever you attend graduate school, you are likely to make many friends and contacts whom you will wish to keep for a lifetime, thereby prolonging your relationship with the location of your school. You may also wish to consider the benefits of studying in a city where you would like to be employed after graduation. Finally, be careful of the "spouse factor." If you fail to consider the needs of your spouse, you may find yourself in need of a new one.

The cost of living in the area around the school will have a direct bearing on the cost of your graduate education, but students are usually quite creative at controlling overhead. Even if you have been living the good life between college and graduate school, you can return to a frugal lifestyle more easily than you might think. Cost of living is considered in all financial aid arrangements. In general, cost of living by itself should not be a determining factor in your selection.

On the other hand, the cost of the programs themselves can be quite daunting. Few people know that almost all of the fees associated with applying to graduate school can be waived due to financial hardship, if you allow extra time for such appeals. This thin volume cannot cover all of the specific financial aid sources available to you, but there are many. Suffice it to say that if you are applying to a preprofessional program, future earning poten-

Copyright 1991 John Grimes. Used with permission.

"JENNIFER, I'M QUITTING MY JOB AND GOING TO GRADUATE SCHOOL. WILL YOU CARRY ME?"

tial obliterates worries about immediate high costs; if you are applying to an academic program, there are a host of fellowships, scholarships, assistanceships, and other sources of monies available. Stories abound of professional students who drifted from one Ph.D. program to another, one grant or fellowship to another, for decades. Incidentally, applying for these scholarships, fellowships, grants, and so on, usually requires writing an essay. There are some scholarship and grant essays included in Chapter 6, *Samples, Samples, Samples.* The best source for financial aid information is the school to which you are applying. Here are a few guides to give you an idea of what is out there (there are more listed in the bibliography to this book):

The Graduate Scholarship Book: The Complete Guide to Scholarships, Fellowships, Grants and Loans for Graduate and Professional Study, Daniel J. Cassidy (Englewood Cliffs, NJ: Prentice Hall, 2nd ed., 1990).

How to Find Out About Financial Aid: A Guide to Over 700 Directories Listing Scholarships, Fellowships, Loans, Grants, Awards, Internships, Gail Ann Schlachter (Los Angeles, CA: Reference Service Press, 1987).

Peterson's Grants for Graduate Students, compiled by the University of Massachusetts at Amherst (Princeton, NJ: Peterson's Guides, 3rd ed., 1991).

Peterson's Grants for Post-Doctoral Students, compiled by the University of Massachusetts at Amherst (Princeton, NJ: Peterson's Guides, 1991).

Directory of Financial Aids for Minorities, Gail Ann Schlachter (Los Angeles, CA: Reference Service Press, 1989).

Directory of Financial Aids for Women, Gail Ann Schlachter (Los Angeles, CA: References Service Press, 1987).

Financial aid applications often have an earlier deadline than the application for the program itself, and they sometimes require supporting documentation that will require some time to compile, so plan ahead. Also, do not just accept no for an answer. I heard of one student who was told by a certain school that no money would be available for his graduate studies; when he called back to tell them that another school was offering him a $24,000 fellowship, they suddenly found $24,500 with his name on it. Do not be rude or pushy, but do not be afraid to ask. Then ask again.

Concerning the cost of graduate education, my advice is simple: Decide to go and you will find a way to finance it. Education is an investment in yourself, and it is one of the smartest investments you can make. Education lasts for a lifetime, pays rich dividends, and cannot be repossessed.

THE WIZARD OF ID  **Brant parker and Johnny hart**

By permission of Johnny Hart and NAS, Inc.

Use the above criteria along with your own unique considerations to rank the schools on your list. You are looking for a good match between your capabilities and what the program requires, and a good match between your intellectual interests and what a program has to offer. In general, aim high. Students tend to overestimate their competition and underestimate their admissability. If you are a minority, a woman in a male-dominated field, or someone with an unusual background, be sure to apply to the very best schools in your field. Education is experiencing a quiet little revolution, and after an eternity of discrimination, the tide is turning slightly in your favor. (Incidentally, my recommendation to *all* students is simple and unabashed: Use every advantage you can, whether you are a white, upper-middle-class suburban male offspring of two professional parents, or not.)

Finally, be sure to apply for the most prestigious scholarships available to you, such as the renowned Rhodes, Watson, Fulbright, and Marshall programs. Although the competition is stiff, you cannot win if you do not apply. Application to these programs is usually administered by your undergraduate college or university. Contact the office of your academic dean. You can also write for more information to:

Rhodes
Office of the American Secretary
Rhodes Scholarship Trust
Pomona College
Claremont, CA 91711

Fulbright
Council for International Exchange of Scholars
3400 International Drive NW
Washington, DC 20008-3097

Watson
The Thomas J. Watson Foundation
217 Angell Street
Providence, RI 02906

Marshall Scholarships
British Information Service
843 3rd Avenue
New York, NY 10022

In subsequent chapters, it is assumed that you have selected and ranked a group of viable graduate programs, and the focus of the material from this point on is entirely on how to get in. There is no one formula that all successful applicants have followed, but applicants who are consistently successful, who win scholarships and grants and admission to several of their first-choice schools, tend to use most of the strategies and follow most of the guidelines presented to you in the following chapters.

■ CHAPTER 2 ■

PLANNING AND MANAGING YOUR APPLICATION PROCESS

Applying to a graduate program requires more than typing up the application and writing an interesting essay. You must successfully orchestrate a number of independent assignments so that they are all completed ahead of the application deadline. Some of the major components of your application process are:

- taking the appropriate standardized graduate admissions test(s),
- getting the test scores forwarded to your schools of interest,
- obtaining multiple letters of recommendation from faculty members and other busy people,
- obtaining transcripts from all your schools of record,
- drafting, rewriting, and polishing a compelling statement of purpose,
- typing up the application form without any errors,
- sending your materials to your target schools via a guaranteed carrier,
- and verifying all of the above.

As you get catalogs and application packets, write each program's application deadline in big, scary letters on the outside of the envelope. You will want to turn in all your materials *at least* four weeks before this deadline, so write "target deadline: one month prior" on the envelope under the deadline.

> Deadline: a) a clearly marked line around prisoner of war camps at which an escaping prisoner would be shot to death, orig. U.S. Civil War; b) a date or time after which a story cannot be accepted for publication or broadcast; c) the worst possible time to turn in your application to graduate school.

There are two good reasons to turn your materials in early. The first is it gives you more time to make a mistake. You can send another request for documents lost in the mail, motivate any slow-moving recommendation writers, and fix any disasters. It is always the student's responsibility to make sure that every document requested by the admissions committee is in her file before the deadline. This is reason enough to plan on submitting your application months ahead of schedule.

The second reason to apply early has to do with the other end of the admissions process, and what happens to your application when it arrives. Almost all admissions officers use some form of three-tiered ranking system for applicants: those students they definitely want to admit, those they are not sure about, and those they will reject. If the school uses a rolling admissions process, admissions staff read and evaluate applications as they arrive. The closer you get to the deadline, the greater the number of outstanding candidates already admitted and the longer the wait list. An application that would easily have earned admission early in the cycle may earn a rejection if it is turned in very close to the deadline.

If the school uses a fixed-date system instead of rolling admissions, the essays may or may not be read all at one time. Most often, admissions staff will read the applications as they arrive or in periodic batches ahead of the deadline to lighten the crush of work that follows. Even if nobody reads your essay and application until after the deadline, applications are usually read in the order in which they were received. The earlier your application arrives, the greater its chances of being favorably reviewed by an alert, intelligent, compassionate admissions representative. The later it arrives, the more likely it is to receive a cursory examination by an overworked admissions representative who has already reviewed a large number of outstanding candidates and compiled a sizable wait list.

All of this should be taken with a grain of salt, however. If you are applying to an obscure program that is not swamped with applicants, if you are an outstanding or unusual candidate, or if you have made several contacts with the program and they are expecting your application, then you need not worry tremendously about turning in your application several weeks ahead of the deadline. If you are applying to a highly competitive program, however, timing is simply too important a factor to ignore. For the most competitive programs in the nation, my recommendation is to apply as soon as you can after the school begins accepting applications. Call the school or check the catalog to be sure of that date.

There is no correct number of applications to make. For some of you, there will be only one or two schools to which you plan to apply. This is particularly true if you are interested in a very specialized area, such as underwater archeology or the poetry of Ernest Hemingway. If, on the other hand, you are applying to medical school, it would not be at all unusual to plan on applying to thirty or more schools in a single year. Targeting a large number of schools is especially common in medicine, business, and law.

If you are applying to a large number of programs, it is a good idea to use this bit of strategy. Divide your schools into three categories: top-tier schools, the most competitive; second-tier schools, competitive but not *that* competitive; and third-tier schools, those schools you are pretty sure will admit you. Note that this is a purely subjective ranking. One student's third-tier school may be another student's second- or even first-tier school.

This strategy will ensure that even if you do not gain admittance to your first-choice schools you will still be able to continue with your career plans without waiting a full year to try again. Do not apply to any schools you would not attend. Why waste everybody's time?

(Some students reading a draft of this book pointed out that the three-tiered system presented here is a new and entirely different way of ranking schools than the one presented in the first chapter. They are absolutely correct. My recommendation remains that you should research and pursue educational programs that meet your intellectual needs. However, if you have a large grouping of schools that all meet your intellectual needs, then this second ranking system will help ensure not only that you are not rejected by all targeted schools, but also that you will be admitted to one of the best schools possible, without applying to every single one.)

Incidentally, if you are admitted to several programs, do not necessarily decline all but one. It might be a good idea to write to one of the schools that you do not choose to attend and ask for a one-year deferral. This will give you a back-up option in the event of any disasters with your first-choice program. Also, when you decline an admissions offer, always do so very gracefully, as your future may include advanced degrees, fellowships, grants, and other projects involving these same people. Write to the admissions office, certainly, but also write to any professors with whom you had established a special rapport.

As soon as you know which schools you will be focusing on, take the time to really read the catalogs and application packets. It is now time to prepare your activity log and timeline. Start with your first-choice school. Read the application materials with a magnifying glass in one hand and a fine-toothed comb in the other. Break down the application process into a series of smaller assignments, like the list that starts this chapter. Then, arrange these assignments in the order in which you plan to complete them. Put a target date next to each assignment, and check each one off when it is finished. Warning: Approach your letter-of-recommendation writers at the earliest possible moment. Be sure to read and follow the instructions in Chapter 7, *Letters of Recommendation*. Some undergraduate advising offices have a letter of recommendation filing and forwarding service which will hold your letters in confidence and mail them out to the schools you specify. If you use such a service, it will have yet another set of deadlines for you to observe.

After you have prepared a detailed activity log and timeline for your first-choice school, make activity logs and timelines for all the other schools you plan to apply to, but keep your first-choice schools first in mind. If chasing down an obscure community college transcript for your last-choice school causes you to miss an interim deadline for your first-choice school, you are not prioritizing your tasks wisely.

SAMPLE ACTIVITY LOG AND TIMELINE

ACTIVITY	ACTUAL DUE DATE	MY TARGET DATE	DONE?	DATE DONE
Ask Dr. Foster for letter of rec	Feb 25	Sep 7	✓	Sep 7
verify sent	Feb 25	Sep 14		
Ask Prof. Ryan for letter of rec	Feb 25	Sep 7 (first day class)	✓	Sep 7
verify sent	Feb 25	Sep 14	✓	Sep 10 (thank you note sent)
order transcripts from ASU	Feb 25	Sep 1	✓	Sep 6
order transcripts from U of M	Feb 25	Sep 1	✓	Sep 6
order GRE scores forwarded	Mar 25	Aug 15	✓	Aug 15
send in essay and application	Feb 25	Oct 1	✓	Sep 27
verify receipt and completeness	Feb 25	Oct 5	✓	Oct 5 (except one letter of rec)

The rest of this chapter gives a variety of tips and techniques for approaching and gaining entrance to your first-choice school. Not all of these techniques are appropriate for every student or for every application, but they are all techniques that have worked for others and that you should know about. Some require a strong and outgoing personality, and almost all require a deep conviction and almost total lack of doubt about your educational interests and career direction. If a technique does not feel right for you, do not use it.

~~~~~~~~~~ ◆ ~~~~~~~~~~

As you may have guessed by now, time is one of the most important factors in your application process. Some of the best techniques require extensive lead time. For example, it is much easier to get into a summer program at a top-tier school than it is to get admitted to a regular degree program at the same school. Some medical and dental schools even offer auxiliary summer pre-medical classes open to undergraduates. You must plan to attend such a program as much as a full year before you intend to apply to a graduate program, but the advantages are immense. If you study hard and make high grades, you will have demonstrated that you can perform at the level the school demands. Besides, the experience looks great on your transcript wherever you go. Finally, if you get into *any* summer program at a highly selective institution, you can walk over to the department you are interested in for graduate studies and make friends. This should not be difficult. Just walk over and say, "Hi, I'm Andrea Tipton and I'm interested in graduate studies in cultural anthropology. What is your program like here?" Be friendly. This edge, and the names you can drop later in your essay, can cinch your admittance. I met one American student who got admitted to Oxford by taking a summer enrichment program and impressing the professor.

Similarly, you can take internships or gain employment in your field of interest. This demonstrates commitment to your career goal, and reassures admissions counselors that your interest is not a passing fancy. If you intend to study law or medicine, it is a real plus to prove that you know what the daily life of an attorney or a physician is really like. Applications for summer internships are typically accepted the winter before, and by March the majority of the programs will be full. Summer jobs can be obtained later, but it is a good idea to start making contacts one to three months before summer break. Incidentally, anyone planning to attend law school should read two books, *Full Disclosure: Do You Really Want to Be a Lawyer* by The Young Lawyers Division of the ABA, compiled by Susan J. Bell (Princeton, NJ: Peterson's, 1989) and *Running from the Law: Why Good Lawyers Are Getting Out of the Legal Profession* by Deborah L. Arron (Berkeley, CA: Ten Speed Press, 1991). Anyone planning to attend medical school should read *Medical School Admissions: The Insider's Guide* by J. Zebala and D. Jones (New Haven, CT: Mustang Publishing Company, 1989).

Do not hesitate to volunteer to gain related experience. Volunteering in public service areas demonstrates social commitment in addition to whatever skills and maturity you may gain from the experience itself. Volunteering is also a way of creating your own business internships. Students have volunteered at such venues as television stations and architectural studios to gain experience and explore their interest in a particular field of graduate study.

If you are applying to competitive programs, your activities and honors can sometimes be a deciding factor between admission and rejection. Students tend to overestimate the value of activities, however. It is better to devote yourself to your studies than to explain your weak grade point average with a fistful of activities. In general, quality counts over quantity. It is preferable to be an officer of one organization than to be a member of five or six. Social sororities and fraternities do not really count as activities, unless you are an officer or committee chair. Many students start their own activities, demonstrating initiative as well as organizational and interpersonal skills. Do not ever make up organizations or any other part of your application! Besides being patently immoral, it is extremely risky. Some of the people reviewing your application may have graduated from your school as recently as last year; they may even know you. Schools routinely request supporting material whenever they get an application that seems unlikely. Besides, it is never too late to join the Poet's Circle or to chair the social committee for Students for the Elimination of Xeronisus. There are dozens of organizations waiting for your participation, so help them out while strengthening your own candidacy.

Completely nonacademic activities also count, often more than the routine college-sponsored activities. For example, if you are a nationally ranked horseback rider in dressage, your commitment to excellence in this outside arena will be highly regarded by admissions readers. Any enduring outside passion is usually seen as positive, unless you reveal that you are unsure whether to become a professional soccer player or go on to medical school. If you are confused about your true priorities, your

HERMAN®

"He was the world's greatest juggler."

avocation could threaten your future vocation. Finally, true commitment over a length of time to any charitable organization will make a favorable impression on reviewers. Do not overlook opportunities to make unusual contributions; students have helped launch soup kitchens, performed as puppeteers and clowns at daycare centers, and volunteered for whole summers at wildlife rehabilitation facilities located in the middle of nowhere.

Having your work published is a recognized sign of intellectual and academic promise, and is somewhat easier than most students think. It is impossible, of course, if you never prepare and submit an article for publication. If you are working closely with a professor on research work that will be submitted for publication, you should brazenly ask to be included as a co-author. The worst that will happen is that the answer will be no. There has been something of an explosion recently in the number of co-authors cited on papers, so the answer may very well be yes. If the answer *is* yes, be prepared for an increase in your responsibilities on the project; this is often the price of one's early publications. Most major universities and many smaller institutions have some sort of undergraduate research journal, in which student research is published in the standardized style for that field. The main purpose of these journals is not so much to disseminate the fascinating research of undergraduates as it is to teach students the publication formats and practices that will be required for success later in their academic careers. If there is no journal appropriate for your submission, start your own. Do a good job of it, because it is very likely the admissions committee will ask to see a copy.

***

Proper preparation for the graduate admissions exams requires extensive lead time. They are only offered a few times each year so you need to plan ahead. You need time to study, also. The first thing you must do is order test information booklets and application information. They can be obtained from:

> Graduate Record Examination (GRE), ETS, P.O. Box 6000, Princeton,
> NJ 08541-6000, phone (609) 771-7670.
> *GRE Information Bulletin* (free)
> *Practicing to Take the GRE General Test*
> *Practicing to Take the GRE {Subject Test Name Here} Test*
>
> Graduate Management Admissions Test (GMAT), ETS, P.O. Box 6103,
> Princeton, NJ 08541-6103, phone (609) 771-7330.
> *GMAT Bulletin of Information* (free)
> *The Official Guide for GMAT Review*
> *The Official Software for GMAT Review*
>
> Law School Admission Test (LSAT), Law School Admissions Service,
> P.O. Box 2000, Newtown, PA 18940-0998, phone (215) 968-1100.
> *Law Services Information Book* (free)

Medical College Admission Test (MCAT), Association of American Medical Colleges, Attn: Membership & Publication Orders, One Dupont Circle, NW, Suite 200, Washington, D.C. 20036, phone (202) 828-0416.
MCAT Student Manual
Medical School Admissions Requirements

Let there be no doubt: You should study for any graduate admissions test; studying *will* result in a better score. Take a test preparation class or buy test preparation booklets. Study in those areas in which you have forgotten basic material. Brush up on your math. Play logic games. Specific questions will vary but the material covered on these tests is essentially the same year after year. Be sure to take as many practice tests as you can get your hands on. (Most study booklets have at least one sample test.) Remember, these tests cover a set of basic knowledge and concepts, so you need not worry about truly in-depth or obscure knowledge (the exception to this is the GRE subject tests, which can be rather exhaustive).

In addition to the guides which are available from the various test administrators listed above, there are many, many more study guides available to you. A visit to your college bookstore should be your first step. Here are a few examples, just to give you an idea of what to look for:

Total Math Review for the GMAT, GRE, and Other Graduate School Admission Tests, by David Frieder (New York, NY: Arco, 1982).

Cliffs Math Review for Standardized Tests, by Jerry Bobrow (Lincoln, NE: Cliffs Notes, 1985).

Cliffs Graduate Record Examination General Test Preparation Guide, by William A. Covino, et al. (Lincoln, NE: Cliffs Notes, 1986).

Barron's How to Prepare for the GRE: Graduate Record Examination, General Test, by Samuel C. Brownstein, et al. (Hauppauge, NY: Barron's Educational Series, 9th ed., 1990).

Graduate Record Examination General Test (GRE) by T. Martinson and G. Crocetti (New York, NY: Arco, 2nd ed., 1987).

Cliffs Graduate Management Admission Test Preparation Guide, by Jerry Bobrow, et al. (Lincoln, NE: Cliffs Notes, 1986).

LSAT: Law School Admission Test by T. H. Martinson (New York, NY: Arco, 3rd ed., 1989).

Barron's How to Prepare for the Medical College Admission Test, MCAT by H. Seibel and K. Guyer (Woodbury, NY: Barron's Educational Series, 1987).

A Complete Preparation for the MCAT, J. L. Flowers, M.D., M.P.H. (Health Professions Educational Service, Inc., P.O. Box 34631, Bethesda, MD 20817).

Your test results will be sent to the schools you specify. Some schools do not require a graduate admissions test at all, some require the GRE and a subject test, some require the GRE but not a subject test, even in the projected area of study. Once again, read each catalog and application carefully, and read the test manual carefully as well.

~~~~~~~~~~ ◆ ~~~~~~~~~~

A brilliant technique used by some top applicants is to approach the faculty of a targeted institution and begin to discuss research and study topics. (A very few schools actually request that you name a faculty sponsor as part of your application process.) Most catalogs have some information on faculty members, and you can ask the school for a more detailed profile. Write to an administrative or a departmental office, such as "Office of the Graduate English Department," "Office of Information Services," or "Office of Community Affairs," and ask for information on specific faculty members. (Do not write the admissions office, as your request is likely to land in a black hole.) Not every school keeps such profiles, but often you will be able to obtain a detailed description of the faculty member's education, writings, recent symposia and presentations, and perhaps some press clippings. If the departmental office has no information on a professor you find interesting, write directly to him and ask for a bibliography of his recent writings or for the syllabus to

HERMAN®

HISTORY TEST ANSWERS $5.00 FOR 10

"The court ruled in his favor."

one of the classes mentioned in the catalog that you found intriguing. You should make contacts like this anyway as part of the process of ensuring that you and the program are a good match. This technique is recommended more for academic and research programs than for business, law, or medical schools, although with tact you should feel comfortable using it anywhere. Here is an excerpt from one student's letter to a possible graduate advisor:

> Dear Dr. Herrick:
>
> I am interested in continuing my graduate work in history at SUNYAB. I recently completed my master's project at NYU under the direction of Dr. T. L. I. Fitzsimons (see attached c.v.), and I will be receiving my degree this February. After a brief hiatus, I hope to return to my studies next fall with the intent of pursuing a program of study culminating in the doctoral degree.
>
> My area of interest within the SUNYAB History Department is U.S. social history. I am particularly intrigued by the history of the New Left in the United States, and did my research project on student movements of the late 1960s and early 1970s. In the course of my research, I came across your name often. I would appreciate the opportunity to further explore and analyze this topic in history, as I believe that we all have much more to learn about the American New Left and its shifting place in history.
>
> My current interest is an analysis of the schism between . . . .

Do not hesitate to make contact with a school at multiple levels: with the graduate admissions office, with key faculty members directly, with any student associations you would like to join after admission, and perhaps even through any friends of your family who are prominent alumni. This is lobbying at its most straightforward, and there is nothing wrong with it unless you begin to sound desperate, or are rude or arrogant.

In addition to the materials officially requested by the graduate admissions office, some students send in supplemental items. Submitting directly related materials, such as an undergraduate thesis or published articles, is certainly within the bounds of propriety. Once again, let quality take precedence over quantity. Admissions counselors have only so much time to devote to each application, so a smart applicant will, for instance, send in her *best* article and just list the others on a bibliography. I know of one applicant for a theater M.F.A. program who enclosed a copy of a play he had written. The head of the department picked up the play for a quick look and ended up reading it straight through in one sitting.

He was so excited about this applicant that he called the candidate late that evening and admitted him immediately. The play got the student in; the rest of his application was irrelevant.

In this same vein, an applicant to architectural school might submit a rendering, applicants to film school might submit a student-produced film, and so on. Warning: If you choose to submit a video or film, it had better be very good, and it had better be shorter than ten minutes long. Any visual media should be submitted in the most universal and accessible format: standard VHS for moving pictures, prints instead of slides for photographs. (Some art and architecture programs require submission of a portfolio; read the application carefully and submit your work in the format specified.)

Applicants have been known to submit some rather unusual items that could not be classified as *directly related,* such as a model ship in a bottle to demonstrate the student's detail skills. This is risky, as the attention that you get may not be the kind you want. One very important rule for submitting additional material of any kind is that it should be truly additional; that is, your regular application and essay should be complete and compelling. Do not substitute any unusual item for something officially requested. Follow directions! If the admissions packet calls for a 2½ x 2½ color photo, then provide one; a self-portrait in pastels would be an egregious error. You should be aware that, although some admissions people are amused by funny submissions, far more are annoyed by them.

You should visit your top-choice schools if you can. Although compulsory interviews have all but disappeared, almost all schools welcome visits from prospective students. A personal interview makes a deep impression on admissions counselors, much deeper than an essay and a file full of two-dimensional application materials. However, a personal visit is a risky endeavor, as you may reveal more about yourself than you intend. A successful visit requires planning and due consideration of protocol.

You must think of this visit as what it is, a dog and pony show. First of all, you must look the part. That is, you must look like somebody who belongs at the school to which you are applying. If students at your targeted school wear casual clothes and Birkenstocks, you will look woefully out of place in your interview wearing a new suit. On the other hand, some students at business schools wear a suit every day. My recommendation is to dress one step better than the most formally dressed students pictured in the program's catalog. Jewelry should be kept to a minimum. Try to look clean, healthy, sane, and comfortable. Try not to look rich.

Never, never, never just "show up" on campus and expect to be shown around. Call the departmental office or the admissions office well in advance of your visit, tell them you are very interested in their program and that you would like to visit, and respectfully ask if someone could meet with you while you are on campus. You should always broaden your objectives beyond the main office. For example, you could ask for an introduction to a specific professor or any currently enrolled graduate student, or for a tour of their famous electron spectroscopy laboratory, or some other special feature of the campus or program.

A few days before your visit, call and confirm every appointment. This little act of courtesy is one of the most overlooked, and most appreciated, of polite gestures. It demonstrates consideration and maturity, and also helps ensure that you do not wait outside somebody's office for hours to no avail.

Before your visit, you should prepare yourself to be very articulate about your choice of graduate studies and about your interest in the particular school you are visiting. You should also be ready to ask intelligent questions about their program, facilities, faculty, future job prospects for graduates, and so on. If you cannot do this, you should forgo the visit entirely. Remember to interview your interviewers! If you act like you are interested in a good fit between your needs and interests and what the program offers, you will make a more favorable impression than if you seem like a supplicant begging for any spot on next year's roster. Some applicants even ask admissions counselors to rank and discuss the *other* programs they are considering, but I am not convinced that this is such a great idea. No one is going to enjoy saying, "Yes, their program is better than ours."

The admissions representatives I interviewed all swore that stress interviews were an excess of the past, and that they never use intimidation techniques or trick questions in an interview. Some students, on the other hand, report that they recently experienced such techniques firsthand. Unfortunately there are no good books written specifically about admissions interviews, but there are three very good ones about job interviews, and many of the lessons do transfer. Here are three I recommend highly: *Sweaty Palms, Hot Tips,* and *Knock 'em Dead* (see Bibliography). These are the type of questions you can expect:

- Have you read any good books lately?
- What can you tell me that's not in your formal application materials?
- So, why do you want to be a _____?
- Who was the most influential professor you have ever had and why?

- What do you do with your leisure time?
- Could you describe how you study? What is your routine?
- Could you tell me about a major failure in your life and how you dealt with it?
- What are your career plans and how does our particular graduate program fit into them?
- What other programs are you applying to now?
- What will you do if you don't get in?
- Why should we admit you?
- What makes you different from all the other applicants we have this year?

The best advice is to be well prepared, and then just be yourself. Remember your interviewer's name, sit up straight and lean slightly forward in your chair, and pay attention. Do not be afraid to say those three magic words, "I don't know."

DAN BLOWS HIS INTERVIEW.

English rights permitted © 1991 Ted Rall.

Ideally, you should show up a day or at least several hours early and walk through the campus to find the admissions office and get a feel for the atmosphere. (Of course you will resist the temptation to "just pop in for a moment" prior to your scheduled appointment.) Show up for all scheduled meetings exactly five minutes early. Always have a pen and paper with you in case you need to take notes, but be sure that note-taking does not interfere with natural conversation.

When all your materials are ready—and you have made backup photocopies of your entire application—mail in your application. Send it by registered mail, return receipt requested. This way you will know for sure when your materials arrive. If it is anywhere near the deadline, even remotely near it, send your application by overnight courier. You should not trust any time-sensitive or vitally important documents to regular first-class mail.

After a few days, even if you have the return receipt in your hand, call each program and ask to verify two things: that they have received your application, and that your application file is now complete. *Be very nice to the person who answers the phone.* Get to know this person, as you will be calling her again. Say, "May I have your name please?" then write it down on the activity log for that program. While you have this person on the line, ask when you should expect to hear about the admission decision. Be prepared to be interrupted and to be put on hold for long stretches of time. Be considerate, be compassionate, and be sure not to alienate this communications resource. Many applicants underestimate the power wielded by academic receptionists and office assistants. They are usually highly intelligent individuals who could make a lot more money working somewhere else. You may never actually succeed in speaking with the admissions director, but these people do every day. They can be your allies or your enemies in the admissions process; the choice is yours. (Incidentally, in smaller programs the departmental secretary often does the initial screening of graduate applications.)

Some programs with rolling admission will notify you within a few weeks. No news is not necessarily the worst news; it may mean that you have been "wait listed." Some programs announce all admissions and rejections for the year on a single day, leaving you to bite your nails and wait along with everybody else. In any case, whether the school uses rolling or fixed-date admissions, they will often tell you over the phone in advance whether you have been admitted, wait listed, or "it doesn't look good." Use these calls to gain information about how the decision-making process works, what the competition is like this year, and what your status is.

If you have any reason to believe that you have been wait listed, do something! One student I interviewed for this book was told that he was wait listed at a top business school. They told him there was nothing he could do about it, and that he should not call, but just wait and see how the year's applicant pool shaped up. "When they said not to call, I thought that meant 'don't call more than once a week,'" he told me. He not only called fairly often to restate his interest in the program, he drafted the following letter to update the admissions committee on his activities:

Dear Ladies and Gentlemen of the Committee:

I am writing to supplement my application to Stanford's Graduate
School of Business. Currently, I am on the waiting list for entrance in

the fall of 1988. Because the scope of my consulting duties at Halperin-Smythe Associates have expanded considerably in recent months, I would like to make the admissions committee aware of some of my new responsibilities. Also, please find included four recommendations from my superiors at Halperin-Smythe.

The most important project I worked on at Halperin-Smythe was our poison-pill impact study (copy included), which shows that companies protected by shareholder rights plans (poison pills) receive significantly higher takeover premiums than unprotected companies. As a result of the study, we received an enormous amount of media exposure, including a write-up as the subject of a Heard on the Street column in *The Wall Street Journal*, a first for Halperin-Smythe Associates. Our findings have been used by companies with poison pill recision proposals on the agendas of their annual meetings to combat these proposals, and have contributed to a number of proxy victories. Our study has generated substantial interest in business and academic circles. My supervisor, Richard Vines, and I designed the study. I then performed the analysis, produced the study's tables, graphs, and conclusions and wrote the Methodology and Example sections of the study.

For another project, I analyzed the effects on stock prices of the 255 share repurchase plans announced in the wake of Black Monday. Contrary to expectations, I found that the buybacks barely affected share prices. Although the repurchase plans failed to restore specific share prices to pre-crash levels, they generated considerable press coverage as a vote of confidence in the market by companies whose shares had fallen dramatically during the market crash. This broader effect would be much harder to measure. The study was published as an article in *Halperin-Smythe Associates Quarterly Report*, HSA's quarterly news magazine, and it too has received much interest from both the academic and the business worlds.

In a third project, Richard Vines and I advised Texaco on the reinstatement of their dividend. Dividend policy is a thorny issue for any company emerging from bankruptcy, but Carl Icahn's threat of a hostile takeover made the problem particularly crucial for Texaco. Management had to pay a sufficient dividend to support Texaco's stock price, and thus detract from its attractiveness to Mr. Icahn and possibly other suitors, without depleting badly needed operating funds. We performed extensive analyses on Texaco's peers and on Texaco, and recommended that management reinstate the annual dividend at its previous level of $3.00. On the strength of our recommendation,

Texaco stock rose from the $40 per share range to over $50 per share in a few days.

This account of my activities over the past few months supplements the description, which you already have, of my duties at Halperin-Smythe (see original application). If you want further elaboration of any item, please write or call. Thank you for your interest.

Note how specific this candidate's update is. He is giving specific *new* evidence to influence the admission decision in his favor. Needless to say, his extra effort was rewarded by admission. If you are wait listed, think of your application as suspended on evenly balanced scales, equally weighted on the "admit" and "reject" sides. Throw something, anything, onto the admit side.

If you do not get in, if after all of this you actually do not get in, do not despair. Almost every one of the successful students I interviewed for this book had been rejected from other programs, and many had been rejected by *all* the schools they applied to in an earlier year. The first thing to do is write to the admissions committee asking why you were rejected, and what you could do to correct any deficiencies in order to submit a successful application to them in the future. If you do not hear back from them within two weeks, call and ask to speak with an admissions counselor concerning your letter of such-and-such a date. If you persevere, you will eventually get a response.

If you are still committed to your educational goals, then pursue them. Perhaps you did not apply early enough or to enough schools, and simply reapplying in a timely manner to a larger number of programs will result in success. Perhaps you need to apply to a lower rung of schools. If you applied only to top schools, you might very well have missed an opportunity to study at a perfectly good school without such competitive admissions. Taking an interim degree was the source of success for many of the students I interviewed; for example, if they wanted a Ph.D. in clinical psychology and were rejected for doctoral programs on their first round of applications, they would get a master's degree in psychology and apply again. Other students found success by just taking a few additional prerequisites and related classes and concentrating on getting outstanding grades. Still others gained workplace experience related to their future career. Workplace experience can prove especially valuable for applicants to law and medical schools. (Many applicants are drawn to these professions without a clue as to the real challenges practitioners face on a daily basis, and admissions committees are more comfortable with applicants who know what they are getting into.) One student I spoke with discovered that one of his letters of recommendation was less than laudatory; when he replaced it for the next round of applications, he was admitted to several programs. Finally, I spoke with a few students who thought they were considered "too young." They did nothing whatsoever to improve their preparedness for graduate studies except to live for a few more years before applying again; nevertheless, they were successful in these later applications.

There are too many variables in the graduate admissions process to warrant giving up on your goals if you are not successful in your first round of applications. Try again, start earlier, and apply to more schools.

SO HE SAID, "NO WAY CAN YOU EARN A MASTER'S DEGREE IN ONE SEMESTER."

CHAPTER 3

SELF-ASSESSMENTS: GETTING READY TO WRITE

This chapter is a series of intellectual exercises designed to prepare you to write the first draft of your graduate admissions essay. Do not worry if much of the information generated by these exercises seems, at first, tangential to your educational goals or unlike what you had planned to include in your application. The goal is to build a pool of possible topics and points, most of which will not be included in your essay. You can draw both inspiration and details from this pool, and it will make your first draft flow more easily when you start writing. No one student is expected to write detailed answers for every single exercise in this chapter, but you *are* expected to answer *every single question* at least in your mind. Read and think, and write as many notes as you can. You may even find yourself in the library or going through old labs and papers to find inspiration, but keep moving along so that you finish this section and go on to your first draft in a timely manner.

One of the complaints most admissions readers make is that "so many of the essays seem almost the same." Take a moment and imagine that admissions reader sitting down with twenty or thirty or a hundred essays from applicants. Can you see her eyes begin to glaze over after several essays that all seem just alike? Can you imagine her relief when she reads a first line like this:

When I graduated from college, I ran away with the carnival.

The candidate who wrote this opening line (see the essay on page 69) said absolutely nothing about his carnival experiences in his first draft. He was not planning to mention it because it did not seem "businesslike" to him. He did not want to be different. He wanted to concentrate on his business accomplishments, even though every one of them was covered in an enclosed résumé. Luckily, he talked to a student at the business school he was applying to, and she encouraged him not only to include the carnival experience, but to feature it.

What makes you unique? Different? Unusual? Sometimes the thing that makes a person really different is something rather personal. The following applicant opens her essay with

strong personal information; she grabs the reader's attention, and does not say much about her educational and career goals until later in her essay:

> In addition to my academic background and work experience, my unique family situation has also contributed to my self-development. As the natural mother of three children, ages 7-10, all born in my teenage years, I have had to mature at a faster rate than most of my peers. Parenting has been very frustrating at times, but it has also provided me with a strong foundation of values and the ability to organize myself and set priorities—all skills which will serve me as a Yale MPPM candidate and a businesswoman.
>
> Furthermore, athletic competition has strengthened my ability to set and achieve goals. Several times each year I compete in triathlons (see enclosed award, my only one for 1990), which requires constant, year-round endurance training. Although I have yet to come in first place, I feel . . . .

Aren't you interested in this candidate? Here is another unusual candidate, launching his essay with his most atypical feature:

> I am not one of the many students who will tell you that they have wanted to be an attorney since they were born. I was born in the U.S.S.R., and for most of my life becoming an attorney in the United States would have been beyond my ability to conceive. In fact, . . .

A doctoral candidate began her essay this way:

> I received a bachelor of arts degree twenty years later than my high school peers . . .

With this line, she immediately sets herself apart from the bulk of applicants. In each case, these students have turned something unusual about themselves into an interesting way to launch their essays. However, note the tone of these introductions—there is nothing frivolous about these writers. They are as serious as can be, just different. They will not seem "just the same" as all the other applicants.

Take a moment right now, pull out a fresh notebook or piece of paper, and write down the most unusual things about you as a person—not you as an applicant or you as a student, but you as a unique and unusual person. Consider your whole life, and maybe even your ancestors' lives. Remember to include personal material, even if you know you would never include it in your essay.

(Some students attempting this exercise have said that there is nothing unusual about them. If you really feel that way, then just go on to the next exercise. Somebody has to be normal and average or no one could be unusual.)

As you begin the process of applying to graduate schools, it is a good time to remember who and what your intellectual influences have been. The next set of exercises will assist you in tracing these influences. Answer each of the following questions with at least a full sentence but less than half a page:

- What writers and which particular articles in your field of study have had the greatest influence on the development of your thought?

- Who were your favorite professors in college, and why? How has each influenced you?

- What is the best paper or exam you ever wrote in your major, and what makes it good?

- What do you consider the most important book, play, article, or film you have ever read/seen, and how has it influenced you?

- What is the single most important concept you have learned in college?

If you can think of other educational milestones or guideposts, write about them in the same fashion—at least a sentence, but no more than half a page.

Not all applicants to graduate school have a specific career direction in mind when they apply. Although it is fine to be open to different possibilities, you might think twice before pursuing two to six years of specialized education without any plan to utilize it at all. (Incidentally, do not become a college professor just because you are smart and cannot decide what else to do with your life.) Your next exercise is to define your career goal, as nearly as you can. Consider why you have chosen the particular path you are now pursuing, and make a list of your real reasons for doing so. What attracts you to this career? What do you hope to gain? Write these items down the left-hand side of a piece of paper. Be honest! Remember, nobody is going to see this list but you.

When this list of your true motivations is complete, use the right-hand side of your paper to write down other ways you could achieve or obtain each item. This is a way of getting you to consider your other career options, what they are and exactly why you reject them, and perhaps to reconsider *if* you reject them. For example, if your goal is to be a col-lege professor of English, you may have written, "opportunity to work with language around articulate and talented people" on the left-hand side of your paper; on the right-hand side, you might write, "advertising agency, publishing company, magazine, newspaper" as other options which could satisfy that desire. Is your career choice really the best one for you?

Now, answer these questions to build a historical overview of the etiology of your career choice:

- When did you first become interested in your current career direction? How has that interest evolved?
- When, as exactly as you can say, did you become sure of this career choice? What event or thought precipitated that certitude?

Be sure to include notes on nonacademic experiences, as well. For example:

- What work experiences have led you to believe you would like to pursue graduate education?
- What experiences as a volunteer or traveler have influenced your career direction?
- What experiences from your family life have contributed to this choice?

Throughout all this, remember that you are building a pool of information from which to draw the first draft of your essay. Can you think of any other life experiences that you might want to include? Make a few notes on them and go on to the next exercise.

Next, consider your academic background. Ask yourself:

- How have you prepared yourself to succeed in graduate school?
- What body of relevant knowledge will you take with you?
- What study or laboratory skills have you honed to date?

■ What personal attributes or physical characteristics would make you particularly likely to succeed in your new career?

～～～◆～～～

What is your biggest accomplishment to date? Take a little time with this one, as it may not be obvious. While you are thinking about it, make a list of "many things I am proud of."

～～～◆～～～

What research have you completed to date? Make a list of major research projects and your role in them. If the research is published, look up the exact citation. If it is not published, devise a working title based on what it would have been named had you published it. This gives a much more serious tone to your experience and is good practice for when you start publishing articles regularly. (Be careful not to misrepresent a working title as a published work.) If you think the work is good enough to be published, get a professor to advise you, prepare it in the correct format, and submit it for publication. You have nothing to lose, and the practice will be educational.

Be ready to describe your level of participation in the research. On one project you may wish to point out that you "designed experimental methodologies, scheduled and conducted experiments, analyzed the data, and drafted preliminary conclusions." In another

After long years of study, Dr. Bing was disheartened to find the speech patterns of the common rat consisted primarily of expletives aimed directly at him.

case, however, you may only have fed rats to the snakes and stood around with a syringe full of antivenin. Then you would want to be more vague about your participation, saying only that you "assisted Dr. R. Simmons on a study of possible medicinal derivatives of venom of the southern copperhead, *Agkistrodon contortrix contortrix*."

It is also a good idea to spell out the ramifications of the research. Too often, students list research without indicating that they have any idea of its purpose. Link your inquiry into the light sensitivity of a certain barnacle to a possible treatment for a class of allergies and the reader will be more impressed.

Finally, list what you *really* learned from the research. Perhaps you gained specific knowledge of a concept, a technique, how to work with others, or even an emotion. For instance, you could have learned compassion, empathy, or even humility.

〜〜〜〜 ◆ 〜〜〜〜

You have already noted the major writers in your field and how they have influenced your development. Can you add any professors currently associated with your targeted school? The following excerpt is from a successful application for a scholarship offered by the Urban Land Institute (ULI). Needless to say, the gentleman named was, at the time, on the ULI board of directors.

> I had the good fortune to hear Jon Q. Reynolds speak in a lecture this semester. At the end of his presentation, a student asked, "Do you see land development as a right or as a privilege?" Mr. Reynolds replied that it is a responsibility. I share this opinion; because of the longevity of land use and development decisions, they must be undertaken with a sense of responsibility to the public and to the future as well as to the investor. These decisions also. . . .

An important note about this type of citation: You must be totally sincere or the reader can smell it. If you cannot be honest in your use of another's name, then do not mention it at all. Do try to avoid featuring the most reviled professor in the program, or the great leader who left last year; you need to know politics as well as names.

Another type of "name dropping" involves minority-related organizations. If you are a minority and you want to mention it in your essay, you need not say anything outright. You can mention your participation in the 1991 African-American Student Conference or your membership in the Asian Political Caucus somewhere in your essay. Such affiliation does not explicitly state that you are a member of said minority, but in the unofficial admissions code it amounts to the same thing. (If you are Caucasian and you have the desire to go out and raise funds for the United Negro College Fund just so you can mention it in your essay, then go for it; raise at least a thousand dollars, maybe ten thousand.)

Names of influential people can be a powerful additive to any essay. They must, however, be used with honesty, sincerity, and tact. The worst type of name dropping is "coattail riding." This is when the student's essay features his prominent father and all he has done for the school to which the student is applying. If you mention someone such as a prominent father, write about him as *your* father, discussing his influences on *you*. That is entirely appropriate if you mean what you say. Make a list of the names you might want to work into your essay, but do not make any firm plans yet as to what you want to include or not.

Students routinely "hide" information that members of the admissions committee would certainly consider pertinent. This is almost always a misguided approach. For example, one applicant to law school developed an undistinguished essay that failed to mention the fact that her father was a superior court judge. Her counselors told her to rewrite the essay including her father. She crafted an incredibly powerful new essay centering on how her father used to drive her to tears in dinner-table debates, and how she grew to challenge her father and win, using his own rules of logic and argument.

Similarly, if you are applying to a Ph.D. program in clinical psychology and your father was hospitalized off and on all during your childhood with bipolar manic depressive disease, let the admissions committee know how this influenced your life and your educational choices. If your mother is CEO of a conglomerate, discuss her influence on your theories about business. Do not leave out the obvious. Remember, one of the authors of your recommendation letters may mention it anyway.

If you feel compelled to hide pertinent information from committee members, ask yourself why. Whatever you are afraid of can and should be turned to your advantage. Take a few notes on information from your background that the committee would obviously consider pertinent, if they only knew about it.

Finally, consider the future as well as the past:

- What are your specific career plans?
- How will graduate education facilitate those plans?
- What is your five-year goal? Your ten-year goal?
- Will you be pursuing additional education beyond the program you are applying to now?

Envision as specific a future as you can, then write a few lines on where you see yourself going. If you cannot do this exercise comfortably, do not force it. Many, many top students cannot see a specific career future for themselves.

As you have probably guessed by now, the miscellaneous notes you have been collecting throughout this chapter are, in fact, the basis for your essay. You may have painlessly drafted most of your essay without realizing it, and need only to string your notes together, or you may choose one single note and build your entire essay around it. Or, in a few rare cases, you may end up throwing all of these notes away and writing something entirely new. In any case, if you have been thinking as you read this chapter, the self-assessment process *has* prepared you to write the first draft of your essay.

■ CHAPTER 4 ■

YOUR FIRST DRAFT,
FROM YOUR HEART ONTO THE PAGE

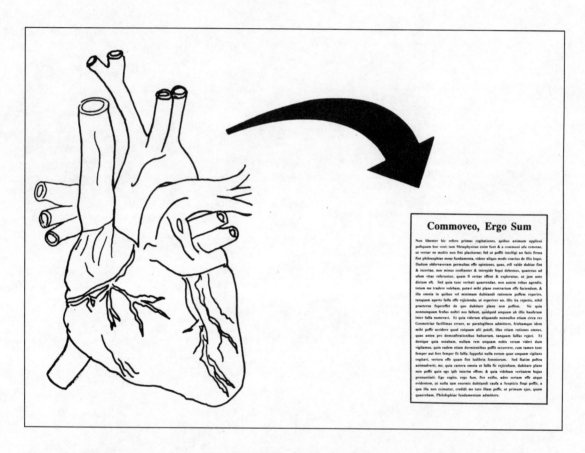

One nice thing about graduate admissions essays is the topic is usually specified by the school to which you are applying. The wording may vary, but the topic is usually some version of "Where are you coming from? Why are you coming here? Where are you going?" Although most schools ask essentially the same questions, they each ask them in a slightly different way. Because of this, plan to write the essay for your first-choice school first, then modify it as needed for your other targeted schools. As a general rule, do not mail in your first-choice school's application until you have finished three complete applications. Some of the ideas you use in other essays can help you fine-tune the application to your first-choice school.

The first thing to do is RTGDQ. One of my teachers in high school had a big rubber stamp, "RTGDQ," which he claimed stood for "Read The Gosh Darn Question." No matter how eloquent your exam answer was, if you failed to address the question directly you could expect the dreaded RTGDQ to appear in your blue book. So open the application or catalog to the exact wording of the essay question, and **RTGDQ**. Then answer it. Truthfully.

Your first draft should be totally, brutally honest. Do not try to second guess your reader at all. Every sentence should come straight from your heart. Write like you talk, using straightforward language. Tape record your first draft, or pretend you are writing a letter to a friend, if it will help you simplify your language. Keep the emphasis on content not style, avoid pseudo-academese, and don't think too much.

Copyright 1991 Kirk Anderson. Used with permission.

Write when you write, edit when you edit. In this chapter you will write, and in the next chapter you will edit. Do not let anybody tell you what to write, and do not let anybody see your first draft; read the next chapter and complete a second draft before you show your work to anyone. The first rule of brainstorming is to fill the blackboard with ideas before evaluating any of them; as you draft your essay, do not critique it. Just keep writing and moving forward.

As general rules of style, avoid footnotes, forgo quotes from people who are dead, and minimize narrative exposition. Narrative exposition is that style of writing you learned in high school: "Should the student feel compelled to build labyrinthine semantical structures, and thereby disguise the relationship between modalities of meaning and the true self, ..."

Be confident in your writing. Assume that you will be admitted.

An interesting first line or paragraph is a gift to your reader. If you are applying to a highly competitive preprofessional program, you will want to pay particular attention to your opening line or paragraph. You have already seen some interesting opening paragraphs in the last chapter. If you are an unusual candidate, or anyone who has had an unusual experience, launching your essay on that note can be a good idea. One candidate told me her goal was to tell who she was in one sentence. She wrote, "I am the sixth of seven children from a large blue-collar Irish-Catholic family in the Midwest." Another candidate wrote, "I am a Puerto Rican woman." The rich simplicity of that sentence still strikes me to the marrow.

One of the best types of opening paragraph relates an epiphany. This can be the moment you decided to pursue your current goals, or the moment you discovered just what it meant to pursue those goals. Here are two epiphany openings:

> I made an "A" in labor relations, but I learned more about labor-management issues in one summer working on a union construction crew than I learned in the class . . .

> When the old man urinated on my leg, it ran down my pants and into my shoe. I could not let go of him, as I was holding him up, trying to move him from a wheelchair onto the bed. That's when I realized that medicine was not going to be just starched white lab coats and golf at four . . .

Use vivid language, the sort that the above entry so clearly demonstrates. Would you not agree that this opening beats the heck out of "I always wanted to be a doctor because I like science and I want to help people"? Just for the record, this candidate's essay conveys exactly that message—I like science and I want to help people—but the writer conveys this message through a series of vignettes employing vivid language.

Avoid using words like these in your essay: meaningful, challenging, beautiful, wonderful, invaluable, rewarding. Say what you really mean; either describe the event in question, or report your emotions and thoughts in more basic detail. Replace these vague words with

a personal statement, something from your own unique point of view. If you have difficulty with this, start sentences with "I": "I felt . . ." "I realized . . ." "I saw that . . ."

Some candidates take a bold position in their first few lines, implicitly promising their readers that there will be more to follow. Here are two examples:

> "Why in the world do you want to go to law school? Heaven knows we don't need any more lawyers." Having worked for the large, prestigious law firm of Bells & Motley since mid-July, it continues to surprise me how frequently I have been asked that particular question . . .

> Learning outside in a 9,000-acre forest was more engaging and exciting than sitting in a lab waiting for some bacteria to grow . . .

You do not need a fancy opening, but if one comes naturally to you, use it. Do not spend all day writing first lines; keep moving along.

As your essay progresses, be sure to RTGDQ over and over again, and address the questions as asked, in the order asked. Be specific and provide details, details, details. You will discover that this approach to writing favors qualitative analysis over quantitative listings. In other words, it is far better to give a rich description of one incident than to cram your essay full of activities and accomplishments without any hint of what they meant to you, your motivations for doing them, what you learned from them, and what emotions they evoked in you during the process.

Do not be overly redundant with other parts of your application. For example, your complete work history may be listed somewhere else on the application, so mention a particular job, a particular accomplishment, or a particular supervisor, only to give a new perspective or to let the committee know what one of these has meant to you personally. However, you should refer the reader to other parts of your application when they are important. Hint that there is far more to you than you have room to discuss in this short essay. Tie your essay to the rest of your application with notes like these: "See letter of recommendation," "See résumé," "See bibliography for additional articles," "See awards." You will notice this technique in many of the essays selected for this book.

Demonstrate that you have read the catalog carefully, researched the program, and considered your reasons for applying to this particular school. Find a common thread, a point at which your philosophy and theirs meet in happy confluence, as in these two examples:

> I was especially impressed by Dean Jaedicke's statement in your brochure that the school "strives to imbue students with a sense of 'incompleteness.'" At Reed we called it "learning how to learn," and finding out how much I don't know was the most valuable lesson I left Reed with.

> I want to enroll in the program at [major university] because of its excellent reputation in real estate and urban land economics; I have not found such strength at other M.B.A. programs. I am also familiar with the admirable work of the Center for Real Estate and Urban Economics, and I particularly look forward to working with Professors Edelstein, Rosen, and Wallace.

I like reductionism: (1) it is efficient, (2) it shows clarity of thought, (3) it is accessible to the reader, (4) it makes for an easy transition from notes to paragraphs. The previous sentence is an example of reductionism, as is the following paragraph:

> I of course know of the reputation of Tufts, which led me to investigate the school. The primary factors drawing me to apply are: (1) opportunity for clinical contact from the very first year, (2) opportunity for small group learning, (3) the "selectives" (pre-electives, as I understand it) available to first- and second-year students, (4) possibility of taking M.P.H.-related electives or joining the M.D./M.P.H. program, (5) opportunity for overseas assignment from the International Affairs Office.

A whole essay full of such paragraphs would feel disjointed, however, so use this technique sparingly.

After you have addressed the specific questions asked by the admissions committee, you are free to weave in any specific additional points you may wish to impart. Check over all of your notes from the last chapter. Once you have given them what *they* want you can give them what *you* want. Think of this as phase two of your first draft.

Whether they ask you to do it or not, substantiating your dedication to your career goal often makes for a strong essay. Saying you have "always wanted to be a _____" is not as convincing as reporting specific actions that demonstrate the truth of that statement. Similarly, it is a good idea to demonstrate that you understand the real challenges and drawbacks to both the course of study and the eventual career you have chosen. Admissions committees are reluctant to admit candidates to rigorous programs leading to demanding careers if the applicant seems not to have a clear idea of what lies ahead. Dropout, burnout, chronic fatigue, divorce, alcoholism, drug abuse, and suicide plague certain professions in staggering proportions, and these problems are exacerbated when people join these professions for the wrong reasons. If you have a real understanding of what your life will be like (a) as a graduate student, (b) as a trainee in this new profession, and (c) as a skilled practitioner, then you might choose to convey this to the admissions committee.

Although many essay questions do not require you to delineate your future career plans, a student with logical, clearly defined career plans often comes across as mature and directed. Your image of your future career goals and anticipated contributions to your field and society in general may be of interest to admissions readers, especially when you seem to have a mission. Think of this as the "purpose" part of a "statement of purpose."

Some students intentionally put a "spin" on their essays. They may establish their distinctiveness not just by what they have done, but also by what they plan to do. One student applied to a top business school so he could realize his goal of launching a business consulting firm—in Bangkok. An applicant to film school featured his skills in computers and digitally animated images, and discussed his role in the future

of animation. An applicant to medical school made no secret of his real ambition, to combine his knowledge of physics and electrical engineering with an education in medicine so that he could design a new generation of medical technology.

If you cannot imagine what kind of attorney or physician or educator you will eventually become, do not fake it. Your uncertainty will show through in your language, or even worse, your ignorance of realistic career options in your chosen field may offend an admissions reader. If you have a well thought out mission in life and in your career, state it; if you do not, you need not mention it at all.

Occasionally students will decide not to respond to the essay questions exactly as they are asked. If you deviate from the requested format, address the issue and let the admissions reader know your rationale for doing so:

> Please note that I have combined questions A and B into a single essay, rather than submit a separate autobiography. I have chosen to focus in detail on my particular experiences during the past two years in Africa, what I learned from them, how they affected me, and why these experiences have led me to pursue an M.B.A. I believe such a detailed description will give you a better picture of who I am than could a general autobiographical essay of the same length.

A difficult essay technique which is definitely not recommended for everybody is to build your essay around a theme. All essays have topics, but few have themes. A topic is *what* you are going to write. The topic of your essay is you: your intellectual preparation, your future goals, your rationale for picking a particular program. A theme is *why* you are going to write, the message or concept or point that strings all your paragraphs together into a comprehensive whole. Themes could include: adversity overcome, the high cost of medical services in a modern technological world, white collar crime, the role of the teacher, how dance and physics are one discipline, and so on. In Chapter 6, *Samples, Samples, Samples,* essay #3 has an extended and subtly developed theme, that Salt Lake City can be viewed as an allegory for America; essay #11's theme is the true meaning of the term 'highest honors'; essay #12 has an obvious theme, 'why I want to be a lawyer,' but it is carried out with great cleverness and humor. If this approach makes sense to you, you may wish to try it.

If you have faced a particular challenge in the course of your life or your education it may be to your benefit to let the admissions committee know about it. A few years ago at the University of California, Berkeley, a student fell asleep during a preprofessional advising meeting. Her advisor, who had met with her before, was quite perturbed. After the group was dismissed, he awoke her and demanded to know why she had even bothered to come to the meeting. She apologized, explaining that she had worked all night. "Do you work all night very often?" he asked. She told him that she did, eight to ten hours per night, five to six nights a week. "Why?" he asked, now concerned for her health. It turned out her father had died, her mother was an invalid, and she needed to work to support herself and her mother. "Why isn't any of this in your personal statement?" he asked. "Well," she replied, "I didn't think they were really interested in the personal affairs of my life." "Well they are," he told her. "By the way, what kind of work do you do?" "Oh," she said, "I'm a private detective."

Here is how one student introduces very important personal information at the end of his application for an orthodontics residency:

> On the personal side, I have been living on my own since I was 13, when my father sent me to England to boarding school to avoid the revolution in Iran. I did not see my family again for 10 years. I made my own decisions, including relocating to the United States to pursue the superior science education available here. I believe this early independence has given me a strong sense of purpose, especially for someone my age. This experience has instilled in me a confidence in my own abilities, a deep appreciation for others, and a natural and sincere ability to empathize with them. I believe these qualities to be crucial for the successful practice of orthodontics, and dentistry in general.

If you have grades or test scores that do not represent your true potential, you can explain them in your essay. As a general rule, it is better to keep everything positive in your main statement of purpose and submit an explanation of negative factors on a separate sheet of paper (of course, you cannot do this on an AMCAS application for medical school). Do not make long, involved excuses; keep it simple and devoid of drama, no whining and no feeling sorry for yourself. Also, sometimes it is helpful to compute your GPA according to your own formula. Here are some examples:

> I withdrew from three classes in the fall of 1990 due to the death of my mother.

I went to a very strict military boarding school when I was in high school, and when I came to college I am afraid I let the freedom erode my first year's studies. Please note that my GPA for the last two and one-half years is 3.25, 3.68 in my major. I feel that my test scores and my GPA in the last two and one-half years are indicative of the performance you can expect of me.

Finally, I would like to address the issue of my academic career. As you have my transcripts, you can clearly see that I was not especially serious in my first few years as an undergraduate, and you can also see that I have improved dramatically. I have a 3.9 GPA in graduate school, and I expect to continue to do as well in the doctoral program.

I am writing to request that you disregard the first GRE score on my records instead of averaging it in with my second GRE score. On my way to take the first GRE test I was involved in a major accident (see attached police report) and I was very emotionally agitated during the test. I realize now that I should have just skipped the test, but I was in a state of shock from the accident and I was not thinking clearly. As you can see, there is a big difference between the two scores. Thank you for your consideration.

My father experienced some unexpected business reversals in the fall of 1987, and I took a full-time job in order to complete my freshman year. By the spring of 1989, I qualified for financial aid, and was able to drop down to a part-time job. If you do not count the year when I was working full-time and going to school full-time, my GPA would be 3.35 overall and 3.53 in my major.

Although I have always been a pre-med student, I would like to point out that I did not follow that pre-med strategy of taking only "safe" classes I knew I could make an "A" in. I took an overload for three out of eight semesters, mostly so I could take classes like "History of the U.S. Before 1865," "Greco-Roman Religion," "Native American Cultures," "Classical Greek Philosophy" and two years of Latin. My GPA in all math and science classes is 3.78, and I think that is representative of my ability to complete the medical school curriculum.

You may lose more than you gain by bringing up negatives, especially if your rationale is not as compelling as these presented here. Unless you have a really good reason for mentioning weak grades or irregularities in your background, do not mention them at all.

Although you should never be slave to a formula, there is a set of key ingredients that many successful essays share. They have great opening lines or paragraphs. They convey at least a glimpse of the applicant's personality, substantiate specific academic preparation and knowledge of subject matter, and demonstrate an understanding of the challenges as well as the rewards of a chosen career. They often give a sense of the candidate's maturity, compassion, stamina, teamwork skills, leadership potential, and general likability, usually

Copyright 1991 John Grimes. Used with permission.

without addressing these issues directly. Then they go on to show how the applicant plans to use the graduate education in her planned career, and establish that the student has an understanding of her place in the "big picture."

The essay is an opportunity to tie all the disparate pieces of your application together into a comprehensive, coherent whole. Some admissions directors told me that they are not always looking for new information in the essay; rather, they are interested in having the essay "make sense" of the rest of the application.

Remember, there is no one right way to craft these essays. Students continually devise new ways to wow and amaze admissions counselors. Some of the most interesting essays will not follow this or any other formula. However, there is something that all the best essays will have in common: All the best essays will be both honest and forthcoming.

In your first draft, answer each question with complete and total sincerity. There is something about the reverberating ring of truth that cannot be faked and never seems overwrought. You will worry about the wisdom of your responses in the next chapter. For now, RTGDQ, let your heart do the talking, and just write it all down.

CHAPTER 5

SUBSEQUENT DRAFTS: FROM THE PAGE INTO THE READER'S BRAIN

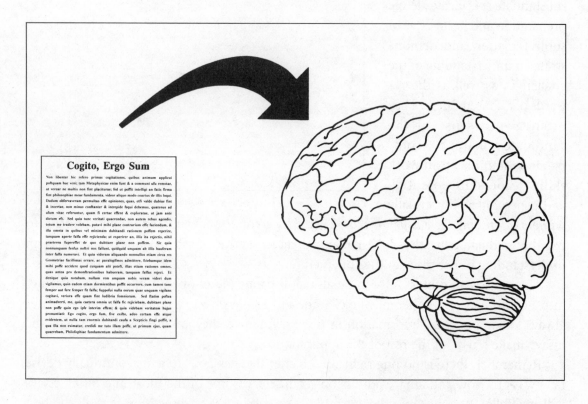

In creating the first draft of your essay, the emphasis of the writing was all on you. This was to ensure the authenticity of your work, that it originate in you. Now it is time to introduce some admissions readers and hear what they have to say. Although you should never forget that *every admissions reader is different*, the following points are paraphrased from interviews with admissions readers at the top programs in the nation:

The Essay Hall of Shame

- "Errors and sloppiness, words and phrases crossed out, even handwritten essays. You have to wonder how they made the grades on their transcripts."

- "Spelling errors, poor English."
- "Anything that starts out, 'I've always wanted to be a _____.'"
- "Sometimes they don't really answer the question. We ask each question for a reason."
- "When they just seem to be saying what they think we want to hear. We can pick up on that right away."
- "The essay sounds like Albert Schweitzer, but there's nothing in the rest of the application to back up any claims of altruism."
- "A whole essay on deep personal problems. The essay should be upbeat, no whining, no excuses."
- "Too long. It shows no discipline."
- "Every year there is always at least one essay from someone who tells us how proud he would be to be admitted to _____, but this isn't that school."
- "Students are so afraid to take a risk [that] they really don't tell us anything. That throws us right back on the numbers."
- "Some students think they can use the essay to manufacture a person who doesn't exist. It doesn't work."

Review your essay in light of these comments. Would it earn a place in the Essay Hall of Shame? Admissions readers are actually quite forgiving—every year they admit people in spite of the above errors. I reviewed one law school essay that had two grammatical errors in the first sentence, yet the student was admitted to Harvard, Michigan, Chicago, NYU, Columbia, University of California Boalt Hall, and Stanford Law Schools. This is because those two errors in the first sentence were followed by an inspiring essay revealing who the candidate *really* was.

If your first draft was truly written from your heart, the material will represent the real you. Now, however, it is time to make sure there is not *too much* of the real you in your essay. Write your second draft as though you were sitting in the reader's brain. In other words, really *read* each section of your essay and ask yourself, "How will the reader respond to this?" The problem with this editing approach is that students tend to over-analyze and over-anticipate their reader. For your first-pass edit just look for the obvious. For example, one student applying to business schools drafted an essay about how her greatest accomplishment was moving away from her family. She had a very close family, and this was her honest response to the essay question, "What is your greatest accomplishment?" In editing her draft, she decided to replace that first response with another one citing her creation of a manufacturing process that saved her company a considerable amount of money. This was not what she considered her greatest accomplishment, but to a business-oriented admissions reader it was certainly more encouraging. Incidentally, one of the best "greatest accomplishment" essays I ever read was not about success, but about dealing with failure. As you retreat from the gut honesty of your first draft, do not revert to entirely safe and boring responses.

Read your essay as though you were sitting in the reader's brain, and correct only the obvious errors. Do not over-analyze!

For example, you may wish to think twice about responses that criticize past professors, denigrate other programs, espouse intolerant religious beliefs, or feature trendy political concerns that have nothing to do with the rest of your application. It is usually not a good idea to reveal that you are singularly motivated by money, although if you are eloquent enough about it, it might work. Writing about your triumph over past personal problems can result in a powerful essay, but do avoid writing about ongoing mental anguish. Finally, you might bear in mind what one admissions reader told me: "I am simply not moved by the claim that someone's status as a Christian is a qualification for medical school."

It is fine to disagree with the entire profession you are about to join, but do not insult your reader with high-handed narrative exposition like this: "Buildings will never make sense until architects learn to . . ." Turn this into a first-person personal statement: "As an architect, my passionate interest will be to improve the . . ." There are many revolutions going on right now in medicine, anthropology, business, and other fields, and you can be part of those revolutions, but not by alienating the first admissions reader you come across. Give her a chance to be on your side.

You may want to avoid writing anything like, "My longtime friend died and after I saw how he was treated in the hospital, I wanted to become a doctor so I would never let that happen again." Such sentiments reveal a lack of sophistication, a lack of understanding of the harsh realities and tough decisions that go with a career in medicine. Read your essay from an admissions counselor's point of view, and see if you want to change or remove any unintentional self-revelations.

Be especially wary of revealing character weaknesses such as sloth, dishonesty, or ego-centricity. Unfortunately, some secondary essays actually ask questions like, "What are your weaknesses?" Try to describe weaknesses that are actually strengths turned inside out, such as "I study too much and forget to have fun," or "I try to do too much," or "Sometimes I spend a lot of time in the library just looking up interesting articles and forget to apply myself to the task at hand." Unfortunately, admissions directors report that they have "heard it all" on this front, and are a little tired of this approach. However, anybody who says, "I drink too much," or "I am not as motivated as I could be," or "I get depressed a lot," is simply begging for a rejection.

Finally, it is very important that you audit your essay for sexist language or points of view. Do not use male pronouns unless you are referring only to the male gender. Unfortunately, it is probably not a good idea to replace a sexist male singular pronoun (he, him) with the neuter plural (they, them), an awkward solution that some have proposed in response to our lack of neuter singular pronouns; your readers may assume that you have made an unwitting grammatical error. Instead, be laborious with your "he or she," "his or her," and "him or her" constructions, as you do not have room in an essay to establish a pattern of interchangability such as the one used in this book. Never address letters to "Dear Sirs:"; use "Dear Admissions Committee:" or just "Ladies and Gentlemen:". The ultimate sin would be to discuss your future contributions to "the brotherhood of man." If you do not understand how to approach language in a nonsexist manner, now would be a good time to start learning.

If sitting in the brain of your reader causes you to throw out the majority of your first draft, you are probably being too critical. This is only an editing exercise, and should not cause you to start over. You will lose the integrity and authenticity of your essay if you write only what you think the reader wants. This is specifically what admissions directors do *not* want.

Once you have taken a pass at the draft using the above methodology, the bulk of the material before you is probably going to make it into your final draft. It will become better written as you go through more drafts, but the points presented will probably remain the same. Only now might you show your draft to another human being, but my recommendation is to wait until you think you have a final draft.

The next editing exercises are more fun than sitting around in someone else's brain pretending to be an admissions reader. First, read your draft for lines that you can "spice up." Try to infuse your essay with another dose of life. For example, "I worked as a teacher's aide at a daycare school" sounds rather mundane and onerous. Using both detail and accomplishment, here is another way to represent the same fact:

> Last spring and summer I was a teacher's aide at a daycare school espousing the principles of Rheikofkian development theory, using only positive interaction. I was commended by the head teacher for devising new games that exemplified Rheikofkian theory in practice, and for reaching a particular student who had been diagnosed as borderline emotionally disturbed. After one semester under my tutelage, this student was able to be mainstreamed when she entered the public school system. (See letter of recommendation.)

If a point is worth mentioning at all, it is worth illustrating for your reader. If your essay is too long, resist the temptation to keep all the points, saying less about each. It is better to throw out some points and topics, and perhaps even enrich your presentation of those that are left, than to turn your essay into a brutish list of activities. Trust your reader to look over the rest of your application and see supporting material, especially if you will refer to it with citations like "See enclosed résumé of additional volunteer experience."

Avoid self-promotions such as "I am an intelligent, compassionate and caring individual." If you feel compelled to make such statements, always use a qualifying clause such as "I think of myself as . . . " or "people have often said that I am . . . " or "I have often been told by others that I am . . ."

If you still have the phrase "I have always wanted to be a _____" in your essay, remove it. You have not always *anything.* If you want to take this approach, try telling a story about the moment at which you first became interested in your future career. Do you remember that moment?

Watch for possible negative connotations that can sneak in with the words you select! Words are rich signifiers, bringing a whole baggage of extra meaning with them wherever they go. If your essay is full of words like "work," "study," "laborious," and "exhaustive," your reader may be tired and exhausted by the end of the essay. If you write, "I practice piano for three hours every day no matter what," you are certainly getting a message across, but a better message might be "I enjoy music a great deal, and I play the piano for three hours or more every day. My favorite composers are . . ." So read your essay again, and see if there are word selections and phrases with negative connotations that you could turn into more positive constructions.

Edit to make sure that you get your message across and do not worry overmuch about the finer points of style. Rough transitions and a few belabored sentence structures are fine as long as you convey the message you want. Do not let your language draw attention to itself; it should be a medium for your message, not a message in itself. Here is how one student launched her autobiography, part of an application to a doctoral program in clinical psychology. The reader is carried along by the story, and the language is plain but efficient:

> My paternal grandparents were Austrian Jews, and because my grandfather was a large and healthy man, he and his family spent the war together in a Nazi work camp instead of a concentration death camp. During the war, my grandfather snuck out of the camp to buy a cow to butcher for his family, a transgression that could easily have resulted in death. Leading the cow back from town, he became lost in a blizzard. Because he survived this night without freezing to death or being killed by German soldiers, he found himself with a renewed belief in God, and a lifetime obsession with religion.

> I tell this story because the result of it was that my father grew up, in Israel, in a series of strict religious schools. He was rebellious, and ended up being thrown out of many of these. His rejection of these schools led him on his own lifelong trek of reading psychology and trying to

find a more humane way to raise and educate children. I can only be thankful that he did, as my own upbringing . . .

Your spelling and grammar should be perfect, however. Absolutely perfect. You should have the final draft of your essay proofread by somebody whom you consider to be an expert in grammar and spelling, but do not seek such expertise until you have a final draft.

Be careful not to edit the life out of your essay. A grammarian and a stylist would have a tumultuous marriage. It is hard for some grammarians to accept, but the English language is like a snake, and it is always getting away from them. The erosion of the distinction between "that" and "which," the acceptance of dangling prepositions, and, horror of horrors, the begrudging acknowledgement that splitting an infinitive is sometimes the best way to wring the exact meaning out of a sentence, all of these cause dilettante grammarians to have sphincter-tightening paroxysms. If you are applying to a graduate program in English, you may wish to be hyper-conservative, but otherwise, write like you talk and take the advice of an overly picky grammarian with a grain of salt. A primer on this subject is *Miss Thistlebottom's Hobgoblins,* by Theodore M. Bernstein. Other good books on style and on editing are *Edit Yourself,* by Bruce Ross-Larson, *On Writing Well* by William Zinsser, and of course the classic *Elements of Style,* by Strunk and White. Your most important desk reference, however, is a good dictionary. If you do not own one, buy one before tomorrow noon.

BIZARRO By DAN PIRARO

Perhaps because it is so conscious and purposeful, the move toward gender-neutral language is not only acceptable but de rigueur today. Other, more unconscious trends in modern usage are less acceptable, especially when your audience is full of academicians. Despite my polemic above, the split infinitive, for example, should be avoided whenever it is not necessary. The early Starship *Enterprise*'s lofty aim "to boldly go where no man has gone before" contains a needless split infinitive and sexist language; it would have been better "to go boldly where none has gone before." Another linguistic error to watch for in writing for a conservative audience is the disappearing subjunctive. The subjunctive is the verb tense which is called for in situations of doubt or improbability presented in subordinate clauses attached to independent clauses. When there is a question whether or not to employ the subjunctive, use it. The French remain staunchly attached to the subjunctive, and even in America, "If I were you" certainly beats "If I was you." In some cases, however, the subjunctive sounds just plain pretentious. As a final rule of thumb, bear in mind what the *Chicago Manual of Style* acknowledged in its first edition in 1906: "No regulation . . . is absolutely inviolable."

Although this book does not pretend to be a stylebook, I would like to warn against two very common errors I ran into in reading many hundreds of graduate admissions essays. First, unless a noun is a proper noun, you do not need to capitalize it. Fields of study, such as chemistry, history, mathematics, are not proper nouns even though they are commonly capitalized in academic settings. Second, the quotation mark always goes on the outside of the comma or period, so this is "the right way," and this is always "the wrong way". If you have doubts about punctuation, capitalization, and similar technical matters, learn to use such writers' desktop references as *The Chicago Manual of Style* and *The Associated Press Stylebook.* Write your essay first, as it is far more important that your creative and intellectual energy be expended on content than on worrying about stylistic details. Once you have your essay, though, be sure that you do attend to those stylistic details— every last one of them. In my research for this book, basic errors in spelling and usage were cited by admissions readers more often than any other specific complaint about application essays. By the way, if you find an error after the application is mailed, it is probably better just to live with it than to send in a "corrected" version; doing so only adds insult to injury.

~~~~~~~◆~~~~~~~

There is no correct or ideal number of drafts, but fewer than three would probably be too few. Once you have what you consider to be a final draft, you can

WARREN EDITED HIS PERSONAL STATEMENT A BIT TOO FAR.

I am who I am.

KIRK ©91

begin to road test it on a few people you respect. Do not be alarmed if you show your essay to six people and get ten strong opinions. Listen to your readers, but do not let them make decisions for you. In the end, this is your essay. If you delete or soften every presentation in your essay in response to criticism from readers, you will end up with a tasteless, textureless mush. Too many cooks spoil the broth, and too many engineers make an ugly bridge. When you think your essay is perfect, submit it.

Your essay should be typed or word processed, and absolutely free of typographical or spelling errors. Some students told me they were successful in running their applications forms through a laser printer; they suggested taping the pages together to reduce the possibility of jamming (then just cut the tape). This is a risky operation, however; if your form jams in the printer you will need to have another application available. Some admissions readers complained about the use of computers and laser printers to make "shrink to fit" essays that were almost unreadable, so do not shrink your essay down to a smaller and smaller type size to fit a space limitation.

If your essay will not fit on the application form, do not start it on the form and continue it on a separate sheet of paper, rather, put the whole essay on a separate sheet and type "see attached essay" on the form. On any essay submitted separately from the application form, it is a good idea to put your social security number as well as your name and to repeat the question as part of your heading. Never print on both sides of the paper unless you really do not care if nobody reads the back side. If your essay is longer than the specified length, you should know that some admissions readers will not read beyond that length (most will, but a few will not). If your essay is very good, however, do not worry too much about its length. Some students sign their essays, which I found to be a nice touch; it vouched for the sincerity and truth of everything in the essay.

Before we launch into the chapter of samples, you need to know of three major cautions. First of all, this book is designed to address the essay-writing needs of a very wide range of applicants. It remains for you, the reader, to adjust the suggestions and information contained herein to your particular case. At one end of the spectrum will be doctoral and postdoctoral candidates in highly technical areas. Candidates for such programs will need more focus on substantiating their intellectual preparation and specifying their research goals. For some of these applicants, an appropriate application may be virtually devoid of personal information.

At the other end of the spectrum are candidates for fine arts programs, candidates for non-subject-specific scholarships, and occasionally a candidate for a preprofessional program such as law or medical school. For some of these candidates, a fully appropriate essay may contain only personal information, or it may consist of just a scene or vignette, providing virtually no information about the applicant's academic preparation and career plans. The samples enclosed in this book run the gamut, and the reader is advised to be sensitive both to the range of possibilities and to what would be considered an appropriate mix of information for her own particular type of application.

Second, nothing in this book should be construed as advocating being flippant, flighty, glib, or "cute." Although I have tried to reveal a greater range of approaches to these essays than students normally consider, I most certainly do not encourage you to write anything that does not reveal a proper respect for the admissions process. Although the other books in this genre often say something like, "and a little humor never hurts," in the essays I read I found that humor fell flat rather often. One admissions director called humor a "high-wire act," and said that he appreciated it when applicants could pull it off, but that they did not seem to be able to predict when it would work. You should take risks in your writing, but take them in the areas of revealing personality, revealing whatever about you is unusual or unique, or taking a well presented controversial stand. If you choose to make a joke, make it a subtle one:

> Whereas in the United States we have great debates about how much and which kind of cholesterol or vitamin to endorse, in the developing countries I was visiting, people die of simple infections, childbirth, nosocomial infections, and even inoculations. I cut my finger badly while in Cairo, and felt the limitations of Third World medical delivery systems firsthand (small pun intended) as my finger was stitched with a huge, oversized needle and no anesthetic.

Humor should be a garnish, never an entrée. Humor that fails is often interpreted as immaturity, and immaturity is almost universally believed to be detrimental to graduate studies. Be different, take a risk, but in general be serious and purposeful.

Finally, do not measure yourself against the samples and examples in this book. Statistically it would be *much* easier to be admitted to one of the most competitive programs in the nation than to be selected for a book such as this. I have selected these particular essays according to two criteria: either I found them to be almost perfect stylistically or I found the candidate to have a particularly strong application, or both. Many of the candidates selected for this book are a little different. One of the buzzwords heard in graduate admissions offices is "diversity." This means racial and socio-economic diversity, certainly, but it also means recruiting people who have had different life experiences and people who have unusual career plans. You do not have to go to Africa or join the carnival to have a successful graduate application, however. No matter who you are, follow the principles outlined in this book, take a risk, and make your best application.

As soon as you are done with your essay, feel free to send it to me, Donald Asher, c/o Ten Speed Press, P.O. Box 7123, Berkeley, California, 94707, for consideration for the next edition of this book. Be sure to include a permanent address and telephone number. All such correspondence shall be considered submitted for publication, and subject to light editing and revision. Recompense is limited to a copy of the new edition. I look forward to hearing from you.

■ CHAPTER 6 ■

SAMPLES, SAMPLES, SAMPLES

The samples in this chapter are organized loosely in order of formality. Some of the essays are for grants and scholarships, some are for preprofessional programs (law, business, medicine, architecture), and the rest are for graduate academic and research programs up to the postdoctoral fellowship level. The essays deal with topics ranging from hoodlums to the chemistry of bioorganic and bioinorganic catalytic mechanisms. You should take the time to read as many of the samples as possible, as you may run across techniques or approaches that are of interest to you even if the essay is on a subject you know nothing about. If a particular essay is not of interest to you, skip it and read the next one.

ESSAY #1

This first essay is a successful example of an intentionally humorous presentation, and you will notice that the underlying tone is quite serious. The applicant's personality is evident in every line, and the reader is left with a grin and one thought: "I'd like to meet this guy." His name is Bob Muldoon.

Statement of Purpose for Graduate School of Journalism

¶1   A gang of street roughs led by a notorious thug named *Muldoon* had virtual control of the San Francisco waterfront area in the 1870s. A San Francisco newspaper started a campaign to end the gang's tyranny of the Barbary Coast, but the editors were so intimidated by *Muldoon* that they dared not print his name. They spelled it backward, instead—changing the "n" to an "h"—and wrote about the "hoodlum" gang. In a few years the word *hoodlum* had entered the English language to designate any street ruffian.
                                            —*Fun Facts to Know and Tell*

¶2   Thus have the Muldoons enriched our language (if not our lives).

¶3   For the past eight years, I have worked at the Travelers Insurance Companies in Hartford. I dare say that I have never been an ordinary businessman. When I began my association with the Hartford Whalers, appearing in the penalty box and at center ice before 15,000 fans, my co-workers were surprised. I wrote about these experiences in *Northeast*, the Sunday magazine of the *Hartford Courant;* at work friends circled around my desk and gave a carnival-like atmosphere to the office. When I appeared on a popular Hartford FM radio station in the character of a private detective named Biff Brandon, they roared their approval. Even my failed attempts to publish a book of humor (Never say "Upper U.S." to an Italian-American who speaks broken English) elicited approbation.

¶4   It's not that I don't take my job seriously. I do. I started in 1981 as a programmer and now supervise a staff of six. In 1986 I received a Travelers Outstanding Achievement Award, which carries with it a bonus of 5-8% of salary, for work in developing an Automobile Competitive Analysis system.

¶5   My decision in college to major in economics (minor in math) was a practical one. When my father, an engineer, was out of work for almost a year as a result of post-war defense cuts, my mother's nursing background eased the financial burdens. She took an 11-7 shift in the intensive care unit of a hospital, but her absence put much strain on our young family (five children). So to me, a business background seemed a sensible one because it promised the greatest flexibility and the widest array of options.

¶6   Many have urged me over the years to make a change, to align my career with my more basic interests. And now I am prepared to follow that advice. In writing, I have found my greatest satisfaction. My published works (numbering 30) have mostly been on sports, but they have chronicled the *people* and personalities of sports, not just the bouncing balls and sliding pucks.

¶7   An intense interest in people—unusual people—has always been a trademark of mine. My mother has often remarked that my friends are a rare collection of oddballs and eccentrics: a 300-pound man who wants to bring the Olympic Games to Hartford; a 20-year-old physicist dead set on winning the Nobel Prize; a 43-year-old actuary with a Ph.D., in his first year of law school.

¶8   "Can't you get normal friends?" she moans.

¶9 I carry around with me everywhere an atlas of the world. Whenever I meet someone from faraway, say Estonia or Uganda, I open to the page and ask questions. No one is shy when it comes to talking about his or her homeland. Volunteer work with the Catholic Refugee and Migration Services has given me the opportunity to meet—and assist—people of different backgrounds. On my wall, stuck with pins like a porcupine, is a map showing where all my friends are from.

¶10 I have long held a love for words and language. In high school, I delighted myself by learning new words from the dictionary. A new word can intimidate, but once captured and tamed, it's yours for life. My interest in writing also has its origins in high school, at Phillips Academy. A framed two-page article of the "Andover-Exeter Rivalry" still hangs on my wall.

¶11 Journalism, I believe, should strive to serve a noble purpose (like driving that Muldoon scoundrel out from the San Francisco waterfront). Surely it must be entertaining and informative, but it can do more. When the Ethiopian famine laid waste to millions in the early 80s, journalists' accounts rallied people. Food was sent. Lives were saved. Long-term solutions sought. Good journalism helps and inspires people.

¶12 That other Muldoon, the original "hoodlum," contributed a word to journalism and the English language. I would hope that my own contribution, if not as great in point of notoriety, might at least be more savory.

ESSAY #2

The following essay illustrates several of the principles espoused in this book. It has a great opening, it provides a rationale for the applicant's candidacy, and it demonstrates the candidate's strong dedication to his goals. It says a great deal about his personality without using any phrases that begin with "I am a _____." Most important of all, it allows the admissions reader to make sense of the entire application; it ties the other elements—grades, recommendations, test scores—together into a coherent whole. One warning: It has something of an ethnocentric point of view. This might be ill advised for graduate programs in anthropology, but it is just fine for business school.

Statement of Purpose for Graduate School of Business

¶1   Alhaji Sannoh's tear-filled eyes, his embarrassed smile, and his small, wrinkled, yet firm hand shaking mine symbolize the successful culmination of a two-year-long international partnership. I was an agricultural consultant for the U.S. Peace Corps, assigned to Firawa, a small remote village in Sierra Leone, West Africa. Alhaji Sannoh was a Firawa farmer who planted rice just as his father and grandfather before him, by burning virgin, hillside forests and scattering seeds. Every week for an entire year I trekked out to Alhaji Sannoh's farm where we discussed the advantages of planting rice in swamp paddies. I emphasized that heavy rains wash nutrients from the hillside soils into the swamps. It is advantageous, therefore, to plant rice in swamps where crop yields are easily doubled.

¶2   We became friends, but eventually it struck me—a painful realization—that my ideas and suggestions were not materializing. My ideas were logical in my own mind, yet Alhaji Sannoh's planting techniques remained the same. Where was the key?

¶3   I decided on a new approach. I leased an acre of Alhaji Sannoh's farm and hired two men. In just two months we produced a fantastic crop of rice. Alhaji Sannoh came to me and said, "If you can plant such fine rice on this land, so can I!" Alhaji Sannoh harvested rice twice that year and quadrupled his yearly rice yield. The key had been his witnessing firsthand what I had tried to convey only in words.

¶4   Two years have elapsed since I returned from Africa and first applied to Wharton. The vivid images of palm trees silhouetted against a crimson sky, and of children's laughter emanating from tiny mud huts, have faded. I have recognized the true worth of my experience not from a romantic perspective, but from a pragmatic one. In my reapplication to Wharton, I cannot emphasize enough the importance my Peace Corps experience has played in the realization of my personal strengths, and in the formation of my career goals.

¶5   My greatest strength, perseverance, has propelled me through an array of challenges. While working with men like Alhaji Sannoh, I encountered an initial rejection, a mistrust in my sincerity and skills, a language barrier, and cross-cultural embarrassment. While coordinating shipments of food aid and agricultural products from the coast to my remote village, I encountered a dilapidated infrastructure, corrupt officials, black market prices, and nearly impassable road conditions. After numerous delays, I traveled to the capital to discover that the village food aid had been sitting on the docks for three months. Instead of reproaching the local project managers, I found a truck driver and bought him a meal. The shipment arrived the following week.

¶6   Because of recent economic crises, Lesser Developed Countries have been abandoning new investments to cope with their increasing debt burdens and depressed commodity prices. In order to be self-sufficient, these nations have to realize the importance of small- and medium-scale enterprises in meeting their domestic demands for manufactured products. They must also exploit openings in niche export markets. In Sierra Leone it really disturbed me to see idle lathes and mills. I often passed one modern jelly/marmalade producing facility that was shut down due to a lack of technical and managerial expertise. Sierra Leone, as well as other Lesser Developed Countries, must set up a national forum to encourage entrepreneurial activity. I want to help make that happen by promoting manufacturing enterprises in West African nations, and by facilitating foreign investments in these ventures.

¶7   Two years ago my Wharton interviewer, as well as managers of international development organizations, suggested that my lack of manufacturing experience would limit my effectiveness. At the time I disagreed, but I set out to address this deficiency nonetheless. I left Washington D.C. to seek pertinent employment. Within one month, I joined a start-up company in California's Silicon Valley as a mechanical/manufacturing engineer. At [name withheld], we design and manufacture an improved intravenous catheter. I have been heavily involved in the growth of our company, from the introduction of a new manufacturing process to the current production rate of 5000 devices per week. Because of the small size of our company, my position has enabled me to implement my own decisions. I have improved our designs and processes and have helped to bring down the cost of goods by a more efficient use of company resources. (See enclosed letter of recommendation.) I take a hands-on approach. I am seldom at my desk, but often on the production floor, troubleshooting machinery, streamlining workstations, coordinating the activities of our six-person assembly crew, and providing technical feedback to our design engineers. Working at a start-up company has exposed me to valuable experiences that I could not have gotten at a larger company.

¶8   My preparation for a career in international development has not been confined to the workplace. Twice a week I practice French with a tutor so that I can more successfully operate in the business environment of West Africa. I want to be as fluent in French as I am in West African Krio, and, incidentally, Hungarian.

¶9   Upon graduating from your program, a variety of options are available for pursuing my objectives. The United Nations Industrialization Development Organization's primary objective is the promotion of industrial development in developing countries. Development Alternatives, Inc., and Transcentury Corporation are just two of the numerous profit and nonprofit organizations that encourage economic development by promoting entrepreneurial activity. Whatever path I choose to follow, I will concentrate my operations in the countries of West Africa and make every effort to encourage their self-sufficiency and active participation in the global economy.

¶10   The last two years have enabled me to view my Peace Corps experience from a different perspective and to gain additional experience in the challenging environment of a start-up manufacturing company. I think that I can now make a unique contribution to your program.

ESSAY #3

This next statement was submitted for a combined program in journalism and international affairs. The applicant gives a series of perspectives on his hometown. His stories and commentary are evocative and provide a clear window into the workings of his mind. This essay has several wonderfully intertwined messages, and is an example of using a thematic approach to writing an admissions essay. Note the reference in ¶9 to other materials submitted, presumably more straightforward journalistic writings. Also note the sophisticated command of underlying intellectual issues while the author discourses on such light topics as an advertisement for breakfast cereal. This is a delightful and impressive essay, meant by the author to be both delightful and impressive.

Personal Statement for Combined Program in Journalism and International Affairs

¶1   Not until I left did I realize that I had been raised in an intensely contradictory city. A city that flourishes on the edge of a dead lake. A city whose center is marked by a monument to the sea gull, the great defiler of its streets. A city of copper mines, green yards, and blue laws. I grew up in Salt Lake City.

¶2   My childhood in Salt Lake was entirely happy, exemplary of a suburban boyhood of homework, scouting, and television. In summer I played baseball, and in winter I went sledding. With my parents and five brothers, I traveled to Fish Lake, Dinosaurland, and Big Rock-Candy Mountain. Our genealogical records were, like any family's, secure and complete in an enormous computer downtown. There was but one factor that set us apart. We were Catholics, gentiles in the city of Mormons. While I always felt welcome in Salt Lake City, this vital distinction between my peers and myself provided me with an outside perspective on my hometown.

¶3   The Salt Lake I remember cultivates its tidy image passionately. It is a clean, well-lighted city. Trim fathers in khaki shorts strut across well-groomed lawns; their wives kneel down on pristine linoleum to tuck stray shirttails into their sons' pants. Supermarket aisles of bottled sodas, cream-filled coconut pastries, and cling peaches in heavy syrup, lead to the meat counter of freshly cut lamb and chicken, the cloying incense of Lysol rising from the floor. Old women wearing rugged cotton gloves pull withered pansies from their garden boxes. At the airport, healthy young men in blue polyester perennially hug their families in greeting or farewell. Such images of suburban paradise are relentlessly enacted in the city I recall.

¶4   I haven't returned there for several years, and I wonder if these years haven't gilded my memories with an unreal quality. Friends who have passed through recently, however, report similar impressions, suggesting the unreality lies in the city itself: a landscape of swimming pools and steeples under blue skies. Serene families, well-dressed, walking to church. Not a hair out of place in the valley. "Is this place for real?" they ask, disoriented, slightly shaken.

¶5   Easily overlooked are the unseemly counterweights to the city's images of purity: Dazzling office complexes have been constructed, ignored, and abandoned. Pockets of underclass have spread around the bus station and through the zones licensed to sell liquor. Stories of a serpentine beast lurking in the Great Salt Lake circulate sporadically. The real monster slithers around the myth of suburban utopia at Salt Lake City's foundation. Frightening figures occasionally surface—increases in the unemployment rate, declines in student test scores, a nonviolent crime rate higher than New York City's—but like the Loch Ness monster, they can never be snared or slain. Does the Salt Lake serpent really exist? Perhaps it's just a trick of the imagination, deadwood spotted through the dense fog.

¶6   To my family, the reality undercutting the suburban myth was quite apparent. Over the years, my brothers settled down in other cities. Even my parents returned to their hometown in Delaware. As the youngest in the family, I felt the weakest attachment to Salt Lake. I left first, finding new homes in European, Asian, and American cities. Yet something about Salt Lake follows me to this day.

¶7   When I was a child, I often saw a commercial that has mysteriously persisted in my memory: A young boy starts his day with a bowl of Cream of Wheat, kisses his mother good-bye and bounds out the door. Whether he hits a home run, takes a grueling exam, or sleds at top speed down an icy hill, a ghostly bowl of farina hovers, steaming, above his head. I found this a bit scary at age six. Now, I wonder if the commercial wasn't prophetic of my adult life. Nine years after leaving Salt Lake, my image of the city pursues me like a demonic bowl of farina. The attitudes I learned as an adolescent, in reaction to this contradictory city—where images of paradise bloomed amidst economic decay—have developed into the principles and ideals by which I live my adult life.

¶8   The impressions of Salt Lake City I have retained are the product of an adolescence spent coming to terms with its culture. From my outside perspective, I sought to bridge the gap between its ideals and mine by striving to understand it on its own terms. I would not realize how useful this practice would be until I traveled to other cultures. In Japan's disorienting society, my childhood instincts helped give me a bearing soon after my arrival.

¶9   Another trait with roots in Salt Lake is my refusal to accept any issue as one-sided. As images of suburban paradise give way to a bleaker reality, so anything wholeheartedly optimistic or ungrudgingly dismal will, I believe, crumble if you poke at the weak spots. I have learned to ferret out exceptions. The desire to express alternate viewpoints and forgotten sides of issues led me to the forum of school newspapers. Even at Reed College, a community of self-described outsiders, I continued to pursue this instinct in the college's newspaper. (See clippings.)

¶10   Finally, I now recognize throughout the United States the contradictions that Salt Lake City so clearly embodies. What defined the city of my youth has come to afflict the country of my adulthood. The blind pursuit of happiness in the face of adversity is one characteristic that our peers in other countries often ascribe to the United States. Japanese economists credit the decline of U.S. economic power to our consumerism indulgences. European intellectuals, notably Jean Baudrillard, argue that America obsessively produces images of invulnerability while its cities fall apart. Like Baudrillard, who viewed it as a microcosm of American attitudes, the Japanese might study Salt Lake City as an allegory of the greater United States. For me, the significance of the city runs deeper. The images and attitudes of my youth there have not only provided a perspective on the rest of the world, they have influenced the principles and ideals of my adult life.

ESSAY #4

The following essay is wonderfully honest and forthcoming, and for several reasons it is a nearly perfect application essay. The opening paragraph is powerful and auspicious, as Leon Battista Alberti is the Leonardo da Vinci of architecture. The applicant puts a "spin" on her essay, featuring her intent to pursue a specialized career and demonstrating how her rather unusual background is uniquely suited to achieve excellence in that career. Finally, her essay ties together the rest of her application in a compelling manner. The candidate has clearly thought about her goals and plotted a serious path. Finally, note the last line of the essay. It is always risky to apply to only one graduate program, but anytime your reasoning for doing so is due to a complete confluence of your interests and the offerings of that particular program, mentioning that fact can only strengthen your candidacy.

Statement of Purpose for Architectural School

¶1   Leon Battista Alberti is my great, great, great, . . . , great uncle on my mother's side. His name is neatly inscribed in a genealogy contained in one of our family bibles. It was only after I became interested in architecture that I discovered who my relative was, although it is common knowledge that everyone on this side of my family can draw or paint, as if by genetic decree.

¶2   I grew up in a lower-middle-class neighborhood in Detroit, one of three girls. My father was a blue collar worker who instilled in me a strong work ethic and a respect for all creations of manual labor. He taught me how to take things apart, fix them, and put them back together again. He taught me to be proud of any job well done, no matter how trivial or how complex. He taught me to be honest.

¶3   My sister is developmentally delayed. This fact sensitized me at an early age about learning to live with disabilities. My mother went back to school in her thirties to become a deaf-education teacher. So I grew up with an unusually strong feeling of social responsibility, of obligation to help others. Instead of being angry about my sister, we responded by "going to work."

¶4   I took my interest in drawing, painting, and sculpting and decided to pursue a career in occupational therapy. Occupational therapy helps teach basic living skills to the mentally ill, developmentally disabled, and those who have suffered a stroke, trauma, or other serious central nervous system debilitation. My specialty was occupational therapy using art as a treatment modality. I especially preferred three-dimensional media, such as ceramics, woodworking, handicrafts and horticulture. I was also taught to use skilled observation techniques in order to develop an activity analysis, or a breakdown of the minute, specific steps needed to successfully complete a basic task.

¶5   As an occupational therapist, I also designed and fabricated adaptive equipment for use by patients. I learned how to manipulate and structure a patient's immediate environment in order to promote his or her highest level of independence and functioning. I designed treatment aides, detachable wheelchair fixtures, and for one client I designed kitchen modifications to allow her to return to her role as a homemaker in spite of her disability from muscular dystrophy (I obtained funding for the work, as well). I have often been the staff member called upon to repair the furniture, fix the ping-pong table, fine-tune the equipment, wire the new stereo . . .

¶6   All of this experience, I feel, will be directly applied in my future career as an architect with a specialty in universal design.

¶7   In my experiences as an occupational therapist, I was often struck at how poorly designed clinic and treatment areas were for the patients they were supposed to serve. In Michigan I was a consultant to Easter Seals on a group project to evaluate buildings for barrier free design. For the same organization, I contributed to a project to map all the wheelchair accessible buildings in Kalamazoo, Michigan.

¶8   At one program where I served, the physical surroundings were so austere that I launched a project to paint children's hospital corridors, wards, and gymnasium in colorful wall graphics. At another program, a psychiatric facility, a "decorator" with good intentions had painted the ward in electric orange complete with vinyl floors to match. The colors proved overly stimulating and disorienting for the sicker patients, and the nurses and I succeeded in lobbying the director for a more appropriate and calming color scheme. I have seen nurses scramble to fill dozens of medication trays with 100% accuracy, while spinning and turning and reaching around in a dispensing room that is only 4' by 6' in dimension. I have seen shower rooms too small to accommodate the patient and the nurse. I have seen grab bars installed at useless angles and levels, door knobs that an arthritic hand cannot turn, chairs for patients that tip over easily or are hard to get out of, counters and corridors that are invisible to the visually impaired (they lack a simple border line; how easy it would have been to do it correctly). So I have observed the pleasures that simple, inexpensive design can bring to patient populations and staff, and the heavy-handed errors that are all too commonly committed by designers who have no real awareness of the hospital environment.

¶9   I have come to believe that humanity will be better served if healthcare facilities are renovated or built by individuals who have some sensitivity to the people actually working in them and some knowledge of patients' specialized needs. I am very interested in universal design of medical and treatment facilities, design of hospice environments, and residential design for the differently-abled and for the rapidly increasing geriatric population. I view these as exciting areas for change and growth in modern architecture. The design training that I would receive at Berkeley, combined with my knowledge of the needs of these population groups, would allow me to bring a unique perspective to my career as a practicing architect.

¶10   To facilitate a smooth entry to your program, I have been taking the pre-requisite math classes (which will be completed by July). I have a straight "A" average in these classes, and I find myself very eager to return to full-time studies. I have selected Berkeley as my program of choice because of its reputation for commitment to handicapped access, universal design, and related areas of modern architecture and design. I am applying to no other program.

ESSAY #5

This next essay starts off with a bold and challenging statement that is bound to alert the reader. The rest of the essay is an excellent example of clear and concise writing. The reader is carried along by the text, and the points are made so smoothly that anyone would have to agree with the last line.

Goals Statement for Advanced Program in Nursing

¶1   In 1981, when my sister Michelle first told me of her anticipated career choice, I was less than enthusiastic. "Nursing," I said with typical teenage disdain, "Why would someone as intelligent as you want to change bed pans for a living?" My image of nurses was one formed by 1960s' and 1970s' television. These sweet, heavy-on-the-mascara fluffers of pillows and minions of doctors were on display in such programs as "Marcus Welby, M.D." and "Medical Center." Such TV nurses were merely filler for dramatic scenes of handsome doctors making profound observations and brilliant diagnoses. However, nursing as a profession and I as a person have grown a lot over the past decade. I now see that the options for nurses are as diverse as the healthcare system itself, and that nurses are finally being given the credibility and respect they have earned.

¶2   As an early college undergraduate, I put aside my original ambitions in art and literature to explore a burgeoning interest in life sciences and psychology. I was fascinated by the intricacies of the human brain. I anticipated graduate study in neuropsychology, and perhaps a career in research. However, I realized that a life spent in a research lab, however edifying, was not for me. I knew that I would sorely miss human interaction.

¶3   Upon graduating *summa cum laude* with a degree in psychology, I took a position as a resident advisor in a group home for developmentally disabled adults. The clients were considered profoundly retarded with severe cerebral palsy and a host of other health problems. It was difficult at first, both emotionally and physically. But in two years I learned a lot about health care, nurturing, and empowerment. Over the past six years, I have worked and volunteered in a variety of social service positions (see enclosed curriculum vitae). I am currently employed as a family counselor at a homeless multi-service center which caters mostly to the mentally disabled. However, as a social worker one is often frustrated by the many limitations of an overburdened, inefficient system. I find nursing appealing in that it provides more concrete, tangible aid. Nursing skills are generally specific, and results more directly observable. In addition, I have retained an avid interest in the life sciences and have been taking science courses for the past three semesters to give myself a firm grounding for graduate study.

¶4   I would like advanced specialty preparation so that as a nurse practitioner I will have more autonomy to make decisions about a patient or a program as a whole. I'd also like to have the option to teach, both inservice at a medical center and at the college level. Working closely with the nurse practitioner who heads the mobile clinic which attends to the health problems of our clients at the Homeless Project, I have had an excellent opportunity to observe her role and responsibilities (see letter of recommendation). This observation has solidified my career objective.

¶5   My projected specialty is adult primary care with a minor in mental health nursing. This appeals to my keen interest in community health issues, as well as my belief in the value of preventive health education and pre-screening programs. I see a strong need for more health education in the population that I work with; specifically alarming is the lack of knowledge on such basic issues as birth control, AIDS, and nutrition. I feel that as a nurse practitioner, I would have greater impact on an economically disadvantaged community. A mental health minor would allow me to deal in a more holistic fashion with the complex problems of this population. Upon graduation from this program, I would like to use my nurse practitioner license to practice in a clinic which provides both on-site services and outreach care. This may include home or shelter visits, or school and community health education seminars.

¶6   I am enthusiastic about your Masters Entry Program because it is the ideal way to achieve my goals. I feel the accelerated pace is appropriate to my level of preparation and ability to perform. I feel confident that my academic and practical background would allow me to excel in the program.

ESSAY #6

Some graduate programs have special admissions tracks for minority and disadvantaged applicants. This essay was for such a program. The presentation was so compelling that it was given to me by more than one person from the school of application. Almost all admissions representatives save their favorite essays for years, and this one certainly made a deep impression. Notice what critical information is in this essay, and how the admissions committee could never have made a fair appraisal of this candidate without it. Can you imagine taking the LSAT as the first multiple choice test in your life?

Request for Consideration under Minority Applicant Program

¶1   It is somewhat difficult for me to claim my disadvantages, as I have spent so much of my life overcoming them that it seems awkward to dwell on them at this late time. However, my desire to have the maximum consideration of my application to law school causes me to overcome my strong inclination to privacy and my natural desire to put the past behind me. Even so, I must emphasize that the material that I am about to reveal to you is, I feel, quite personal.

¶2   I was born into a family of 10 siblings in [name withheld], a poor peasant village in central Vietnam quite close to the border between what was North Vietnam and South Vietnam. Everyone in our village was a farmer, and my entire family spent most of its time in the rice paddy fields in the middle of a civil war. Both of my own parents were illiterate, although they were highly respected in our village due to their hard work and due to their devotion to their family. Although my parents placed a high value on education, because of the war conditions and the critical need to participate in farming, none of us could afford to go to a proper school. I learned mostly from friends and relatives, but with the strong encouragement which I felt from my family, I pursued education with intense zeal. When I was old enough, I passed the National High School Exam with distinction.

¶3   At that time, I was sponsored by the late Dr. Bruce Johnson to go to Belgium to study. Dr. Johnson was a medical doctor in Vietnam as a volunteer with an international church program. Through many meetings with my family, it was decided that I should go to Belgium to study. As none of us knew anything at all about a foreign country, this was a difficult decision for my family. This may be hard to imagine, but going to Belgium from my village is about as far away conceptually as the moon.

¶4   Dr. Johnson's intervention on my behalf probably saved my life. During the late sixties to mid-seventies, as the war really began to escalate, I was in Belgium pursuing my studies. You can imagine the distraction this caused me. My entire village was destroyed many times, and I lost three members of my family. My father requested that I come back to be with my family. I attended classes taught in both English and French. I completed my undergraduate degree in applied mathematics, and my master's and doctorate degrees in economics. Although I very much wanted to pursue a postdoctoral fellowship, I could not deny my family.

¶5   After I returned to Vietnam, I moved my whole family to Saigon and accepted a ministerial position with the government. At the same time, I lectured in macroeconomics and political economic theory at Saigon University. I served in these capacities until the fall of Saigon in 1975. Then I was arrested, jailed, and tortured by the communist regime due to my former prominence. After six months in a re-education camp, I was released in return for my assistance in restructuring certain sectors of industry to the new communist, centrally-planned economy. I despised this work for the communists, but I accepted it in order to gather resources and plot my escape from Vietnam.

¶6   In 1980 I escaped, landing in Thailand after 30 days at sea in an open boat. Eventually I made my way through refugee camps to the United States. I had to leave my whole family behind, including my wife and children, as I considered this venture too risky. I arrived in the United States penniless, and as is detailed in my other materials, I have rebuilt my career with some success.

¶7   I was never educated in the United States, and I was totally unfamiliar with the testing system here. Although I feel that I can be quite articulate and precise in oral or written examination, I had never taken a multiple choice test in my life. Additionally, I had to manage a major consulting engagement while I was preparing for the LSAT. Due to these limitations, I think my LSAT scores do not fully reflect my skill and ability. More appropriate indicators of my character are my career performance, my grades at university, and my service to others.

¶8   As you can see in my other materials, I continue to thrive in spite of my life experiences. Without hesitation I can say that I will do whatever it takes to do well in law school.

ESSAY #7

The following essay has an opening line that grabs the reader by the eyeballs. Notice how much information is conveyed *indirectly* in this essay. We learn that this candidate's social skills allow him to succeed in some very diverse environments, we learn about the candidate's resilience in bouncing back from failure, and we get a feeling for his versatility and energetic approach to any task. Also notice how exact the candidate is in reporting the figures in ¶7: "17% of all revenues," "68 days." This tells us a lot more about the candidate than such direct statements as "I have a good mind for figures" or "I have good detail skills." Finally, what business school could resist someone who had literally won the shirt off somebody's back?

Statement of Purpose for Graduate School of Business

¶1   When I graduated from college, I ran away with the carnival. I spent the entire summer and fall traveling through small town America with Dell's Amusements, playing county fairs and harvest festivals from Iowa to Alabama. I ran what is called in the business a "joint," a game booth, a diversion, a fully independent 12' x 12' entertainment business with a canvas top. Most townies would have called me a "barker," but any carnie would have known me as an "agent." Agents run game booths, and they are at the top of the carnie social structure, as opposed to "ride jockeys," who take tickets from kids but don't really know how to "win money." A good agent can make $80,000 *net* in a season.

¶2   In the American carnival, many dozens of businesses such as Dell's Amusements join together for any individual event, or "spot." The carnival boss, usually the owner of the feature rides that anchor the midway (e.g.: a double ferris wheel) contracts with the fair committee to provide the carnival amusements. Then the boss subcontracts out all the midway space, so many dollars a linear foot of midway frontage, to independents such as my employer.

¶3   The incredible thing about the carnival is that you design, construct, operate, and dismantle a complete independent business about once a week! The carnival is a living business laboratory. If you want to test an idea or a theory, you just do it. My boss soon learned that I was gung ho, and he gave me free rein. By the end of the season, I was running many different games on a profit-sharing basis. Some of the things I learned were: (1) how to motivate employees, (2) how to calculate the odds on a game to see if my employees were honest, (3) how to catch the eye of the customer, 1033 humorous lines to get somebody's attention, how to use sound in merchandising, (4) how to work 36+ hours in a row, (5) that you can make a lot of money 25¢ at a time.

¶4   I had a lot of fun in the carnival, and I learned a lot about people. I won the shirt off a man's back in West Point, Iowa. (I won all his money and then I played him for his shirt.)

¶5   I ran away with the carnival to gather material for a nonfiction book, interpreting this fascinating blue-collar subculture for the upper-middle-class, college-educated reader. Although I took over 1000 pages of detailed notes, I was not old enough or mature enough to have finished this book. I rank this as a failure because I did not do what I planned to do, but I think things happen for a reason, so I have certainly gone on with my life.

¶6   Since I wasn't to be a best-selling author, I decided to seek business writing assignments on a freelance basis. I edited an academic thesis for E. Edleff Schwaab, a University of Chicago doctoral candidate in economics, *The Politics of Sovereign Debt*, on the third-world debt crisis (see letter of recommendation). Then, as a consultant, I wrote a business plan for a restaurant (which was successfully launched), and for one of the largest dental fixture manufacturing laboratories in the United States (a $4 million acquisition proposal). I took these projects into the offices of Rothman, Harbick, Klein, Holst in Chicago (see résumé) and got a position as a junior copy writer for my current employer, a public relations firm.

¶7   My first project was to write marketing material and press releases for a new Mitsukoshi-Bakka mini-tractor for the American farm market. When I saw the photos and the model of the tractor, I called the account representative and told him that the tractor's seat was all wrong, its steering wheel was too small (it actually had power steering), and the whole thing was covered with Japanese writing. He did not think any of this was a problem, but he agreed to let me talk to the client's representative. I bought a book on Japanese business protocol, studied it, and when I met the representative the next week, I presented my position in a deferential way, giving him exactly the arguments he needed to alert his superior. I knew from my time in small towns with the carnival that American farmers would not like this tractor. To make a long story short, the client commissioned a focus group and it confirmed my position. The changes were made, and the client, representing at the time 17% of all revenues for Rothman, Harbick, Klein, Holst, insisted that I become their chief liaison within the company. I went from junior copy writer to co-manager of a major account in exactly 68 days.

¶8   Nineteen months and another promotion later, I think I have done very well in public relations. Because of my ability to "get into" a client's business and understand it, I have been appointed to the business development team. I am the youngest member of this team and the only member who is not an officer. We are currently in a phase of record growth. See employer recommendation. Also see enclosed proposal. I co-developed the concept with the Director, wrote the copy, developed the supporting charts and graphs, and desktop published the whole thing in-house. This particular proposal was the first which I was allowed to present to client management as team leader. We got the contract. I do one or two of these every month, in addition to account management.

¶9   Although my writing skills got me into this industry, I find myself more interested in the earlier stages of product development, in competitive analysis, in the differences between sales and dealer/distributor networks, in the art and science of pricing—than I am in writing marketing and promotional copy, planning trade show presentations, and getting press coverage for farm and construction equipment, a mature line of major appliances, and a regional chain of medical clinics. I may be good at my job, but I feel I have learned all that I can in my current capacity.

¶10   My goal in attending the [major] School of Business is simple. I want to become a business and nonprofit consultant, to pursue a project-oriented career encompassing finance, marketing, and management science. Although I have not taken math beyond calculus as a freshman, I have enclosed my high school transcripts showing that I made an "A" in every math class I have taken since middle school. I am an advanced user of Excel and Lotus (especially for visual presentation of data), WordPerfect, Pagemaker, and the MS Works package, among other programs. I believe I have the communication skills, the social skills, the analytical skills, and the business savvy to excel in a career as a business consultant.

ESSAY #8

Here is another essay with an outstanding opening line. The reader is drawn into the essay immediately. ¶3 and ¶4 contain an excellent treatment of the "adversity overcome" theme. The candidate is matter-of-fact about these experiences, and asks for no special consideration because of them. In ¶7, the candidate reveals his minority status so smoothly that it almost appears an afterthought. It is important to note that this essay is so powerful not because of these factors, however, but because of the total picture of a thoughtful, ambitious, smart, and hardworking individual who is, in all likelihood, going to make a significant contribution to society. This candidate is an example of the type of "rising star" that graduate schools want to be associated with.

Statement of Purpose for Law School

¶1   Even being beaten by a cat has its rewards; it taught me how a personal setback could be used to help others by reforming the system.

¶2   During my first semester at U.C. Berkeley, I ran against 92 candidates in a student senate election only to be beaten by "Bill the Cat" for the last of 15 seats. Despite my disappointment, all I could do was laugh until I realized that a legal problem was involved. I then researched the issue, relating it to a similar case in San Francisco where a candidate ran for county supervisor as "Sister Boom-Boom," and filed a suit against the Associated Students of the University of California with their Judicial Committee. I reformed the elections process by arguing that the members of the association had been deprived of their constitutional right to vote because they had been deceived by the practice of allowing candidates to run under fictitious names.

¶3   That was two years ago, but I had already come a long way from where I was five and a half years ago when, at the age of sixteen, I was diagnosed as being in the latter stages of chronic chemical dependency to multiple agents and sent to inpatient treatment in Minnesota. I was a gifted student who did well in school until, as a result of my dependency which began at the age of eleven, I wasted my junior and senior high school education and failed to develop my personal and intellectual capabilities. I lost interest in student government, community service, and other activities of that sort and received progressively poorer grades in progressively less demanding courses, eventually being pulled or kicked out of five schools during my sophomore and junior years, and nearly dropped out of school completely.

¶4   My regrets for having almost wasted my personal and intellectual gifts drove me to overcome my academic deficiencies. During my senior year of high school, the year after treatment, I worked hard to graduate on time, but because my grades were so low during my first three years of high school, I still only managed to graduate in the bottom seventh of my class. I then enrolled at a nearby community college, determined to earn admission to a top university. During two years at American River College, I completed 62 units with a 3.6 GPA and worked hard to acquire the skills, habits, and knowledge to prepare me to study philosophy at U.C. Berkeley. However, during my first year at U.C. Berkeley, it was still difficult for me to meet the higher level of academic standards; two years at a community college had simply not been enough time for me to prepare to compete successfully with students who had more productive years in junior and senior high school, and, in most cases, two challenging years at Berkeley. Not until my second year at U.C. Berkeley, my senior year of college, was I finally prepared to succeed in a demanding academic program. That year, including a summer session at U.C. Davis, I completed 44 units, of which 26 units were upper division philosophy courses, with a 3.6 GPA. Having practically lost five years of education, I am proud to have graduated from college in four years with a 3.4 GPA overall, a 3.5 GPA in my major, and a degree from one of the top programs in one of the most rigorous disciplines at one of the best universities in the nation.

¶5   Philosophy was central to my personal and intellectual growth, and it helped me to develop many skills which are of particular importance for law school and the legal profession. I learned to process information systematically and logically, and to evaluate it in an ethical and moral context. I believe that philosophy, with its emphasis on reading, writing, and thinking, and its fundamental role in the evolution of Western culture, has not only been good preparation for law school but has also provided me with an intellectual foundation which will help me adapt to a constantly changing world, function well in an information-based economy, and understand the broader context of problems in an increasingly specialized society.

¶6   Even more important to my personal and intellectual growth was my experience outside of the classroom (see enclosed materials). As my community service and my leadership and political experience became progressively more responsible, I quickly gained confidence in public speaking and group discussions, and learned the fundamentals of organization, management and leadership. Working to make changes in my community, in higher education, and within the legislative branch of federal government and the executive branch of state government forced me to accept many of the realities of the political process. Most of all, I acquired a deeply felt appreciation for the freedom that comes with the form and principles of our government, and thus, believing that the real power of government must come from those governed, I came to place a high value on citizen participation in community and civic affairs.

¶7   Even though I have been warned about attaching lofty principles to daily behaviors, I honestly believe that I am committed to public service. When I look at my life—my Mexican-American heritage; my ability to overcome adversity; my appreciation of the educational and leadership opportunities in community college; my education in philosophy at U.C. Berkeley; my involvement with health, environmental, and educational issues at many levels of the political process; and my decision to study law—I see a process of development leading to a career as an elected or appointed public official, where I can ultimately help make the changes needed in our institutions and in the attitudes and values of our society. I will realize this vision of my future not merely because of my capacity for hard work and intellectual growth, but more importantly because of my willingness to assume responsibility, my ability to gain confidence and take advantage of opportunities, and my capacity to grow stronger and wiser by meeting challenges and facing problems.

¶8   For over four years, I have been preparing for and anticipating the opportunity to focus all of my internal resources on demonstrating my intellectual capabilities at a top law school. The size and diversity of the faculty and student body and the commitment to public interest law at Harvard Law School are especially appealing. I sincerely believe that if given the opportunity I will make an outstanding law student and lawyer, and contribute to the educational experience of other students at Harvard Law School.

ESSAY #9

The following essay is simple and direct. In its own style, it is overwhelmingly articulate. It reveals that rarest of creatures, an idealistic candidate devoid of naiveté.

Personal Statement for Veterinary School

¶1   As I was growing up our house was always filled with an assortment of animals—dogs, cats, birds, and reptiles. In the summers I worked on my grandparents' cattle ranch in Central Oregon, and there I participated in the planting, irrigating, and haying operations. My true preference, however, was working with the livestock. I rode on the cattle drives and helped in the brandings (which included dehorning, vaccinating, and castrating). Through these experiences I came to understand the relationship between rancher and livestock, and the often harsh reality of animal husbandry.

¶2   At my grandparents', too, I became interested in horses. My first horse was an unbroken quarter horse, who quickly educated me on the trials of owning a large animal. I have owned two other horses, both thoroughbreds, which I trained, showed, and later sold. As a horse owner I have experienced my share of colics, wire cuts, and mysterious lameness, as well as learned how to handle and cajole an animal that weighs eight to ten times more than I do. I have taught English and Western lessons, anatomy, general horsemanship, and first aid to Sierra Club members and summer camp children, and have been responsible for the care of fifteen lesson horses. No matter what the experience, the companionship, enjoyment, and sense of responsibility I have gained from growing up around animals has convinced me that veterinary medicine offers me a way to combine my love for animals with my interest in biological science.

¶3   More recent events have also directed me towards a career in veterinary medicine. After graduating from Duke with a bachelor's degree in biology, I accepted a four-month internship near Naples, Florida, working at a wild animal rehabilitation clinic. In contrast to my experiences with domesticated animals, the wild animals I encountered did everything in their power to flee or fight their way to freedom. We worked in cooperation with local veterinarians to provide emergency care to injured wildlife, nursing care to convalescing animals, and physical therapy to animals that were potentially releasable. I participated in all aspects of these procedures and gained invaluable experience handling raptors, seabirds, and other native species. My daily responsibilities included medicating, weighing, rescuing, and providing emergency care, as well as preparing food, cleaning cages, and answering public inquiries.

¶4   My internship ended in January and I moved back to Seattle, where I was hired by a major dog and cat hospital. The hospital provides general and specialized veterinary services, employing an oncologist, a neurologist, a radiologist, and an internist. When I started at the clinic my responsibilities included restraining animals during procedures, cleaning cages, and medicating hospitalized cases. I now am the technician to Dr. Verna Petrakis, the neurology specialist (see letter of recommendation), and my duties include placing IV catheters, drawing blood, monitoring animals under anesthesia, and preparing for joint/spinal taps and myelograms. In addition, I have been trained to operate a CAT scan, which the hospital is fortunate enough to own.

¶5   In my present position I am not only learning new procedures and techniques, but also I am gaining experience in seeing how a veterinary clinic operates. I realize that in order to maintain high professional standards it takes solid managerial and financial skill. The hospital only runs smoothly when inventory is well stocked, kennels well maintained, and a positive rapport exists between the clinic and clientele. Based upon conversations I have had with veterinarians and on my own observations, I sense that the profession of veterinary medicine is undergoing rapid change. Advancements (in both human and animal medicine) have created new dilemmas for veterinarian and client. While care has improved and previously incurable conditions can now be treated, the costs for such procedures can be prohibitive. I believe veterinarians must approach their clients honestly when discussing the benefits and costs of treatments and offer alternatives to the client whenever possible.

¶6   After working in several areas of the animal care industry, I have begun to narrow down my potential career goals. While I enjoy working with small animals, my interests really lie with large ones. My experiences working in Central Oregon have enforced my desire to work in a rural area and treat livestock. I am also interested in wildlife and marine mammal medicine. In addition to my work in the small animal clinic, I work as an ecology teacher on a research vessel on Puget Sound. This experience has reinforced my commitment to environmental issues. Wildlife veterinary medicine seems to me to offer a way I can help preserve wildlife and fulfill my own professional goals.

ESSAY #10

If it were not for the unusual nature of the experiences and the personality revealed little by little with each passing paragraph, this next essay would run the risk of being a list of activities. As a travelogue in application for a grant to travel, however, it works rather well. By the end of the material, the reader has a great deal of confidence in the candidate as a traveler and as a scholar with integrity.

Personal Statement for the Watson Fellowship

¶1   After high school I took a job as one of the first females on a 20-person forest fire-fighting crew. In the autumn I attended [name withheld] University where I became disillusioned with college life. After another summer on the fire crew, I spent my earnings overseas.

¶2   Shortly after my nineteenth birthday, I hitchhiked through the South Pacific and Indonesia with a friend. We did a lot of hiking and worked in several towns. I gained independence and strength; I came to appreciate a tremendous diversity of people.

¶3   I returned home and transferred to another college. That winter I started a women's soccer team, began writing poetry and prose, tutored foreign students, and held a depressing but eye-opening job in a nursing home. The following summer I returned to the fire crew, was promoted to foreman, and earned enough money to plan a trip through Asia and the Orient.

¶4   As I traveled through Asia, I grappled with difficult ethical questions. People cheated me; I was plagued by questions, beggars, and propositions. I wanted to experience Asian ways and leave Western values and habits behind. I felt that an open mind would enhance the experience of travel. But in the poor countries of Asia, blonde hair and light skin spell "rich tourist." I found this stereotype and the accompanying behaviors difficult to deal with.

¶5   I also had to deal with the draining effects of illness in remote areas while trekking hundreds of miles over an 18,000-foot pass in the Himalayas. I learned to deal with language barriers, with the frustrations of appealing to legal systems that seemed incapable of adjusting to foreigners. Especially in India, I learned perseverance and patience.

¶6   In the Orient I came to know the Chinese people; I was amazed and saddened that what little I had learned in school about the green- and blue-clothed, bicycle-riding citizens of China, their culture and their land, was labeled under "Communism." I was enthralled with the quiet, unpretentious Chinese people and their vast country.

¶7   In China I met a traveler who had snuck into Tibet when the borders were still closed. My affection for the Chinese people, and this traveler's hate for Chinese rule in Tibet, stimulated my interest in Tibetan Buddhism and the recent changes in Tibet. I was frustrated that I could not visit Tibet.

¶8   After almost a year abroad, I returned home and joined a friend for a car trip to Baja California. Inside a car, I missed interacting with the native people; I learned that traveling by foot or bicycle from village to village is the best way for me to experience different cultures.

¶9   For the next two summers I was employed as a forest worker, working and living independently in the wilderness. In my time off, I took up rock climbing, mountaineering, and snorkeling. In the winter I attended and graduated from a junior college. Then I began a year-long internship in Alaska, where I worked as a health education intern. I also worked in cold storage, on a fishing boat, and as recreation coordinator in a health camp set up for Tlingit Indian youths with alcoholic parents. Among the Alaskan natives I had my first good look at a group of people who were on the fringes of health and stability in my own wealthy society.

¶10   Between camp sessions I began cycle-touring with a 350-mile, two-week trip from Haines to Skagway. Then the following spring I invited a young friend to join me to cycle up the Alcan Highway from Seattle to Alaska; we took two months to traverse the roughly 2000 miles. Besides looking out for my seventeen-year-old companion, I was challenged with frostbite, desolate stretches of road, and a snow-bound 7000-foot pass in the Rocky Mountains. But I met many wonderful people and enjoyed desolate and beautiful parts of North America.

¶11   I also embarked on two month-long kayak trips along the coast of Southeast Alaska. On one trip I tried living off the land; I carried only one sack of rice in case of an emergency. I was often hungry, but I found interesting things to eat—even more interesting than some of the dishes I sampled in Hong Kong.

¶12   That fall I entered Reed College, majoring in International Studies. My extracurricular activities have been performing as a folk musician, playing soccer, cycling, marketing my poetry and prose, and continuing to meet interesting people from all walks of life. This year I am also a house advisor, jointly responsible for 24 students, over half of which are in their first year of college life.

¶13   Reed has been a perfect school for me, and my former reservations toward formalized education have been erased. Academically, I am focusing on China; I am studying late traditional China, modern China, and Chinese history, culture, and government. I am especially interested in policies and ideologies concerning China's interactions with Tibet, the demise of Tibetan Buddhism, and recent rebellions in Tibet. My thesis will be on Tibetan Buddhism and the problem of Chinese rule in Tibet with regard to justice and international law.

¶14   All the religions of China hold special interest for me. I have been interested in religions since grade school. It has continued to fascinate me that religious beliefs are so powerful and influential, yet so diverse and mutually exclusive. While traveling, I read books about the religions of each country I visited; Buddhism in India especially interested me. I have studied the sociology of religions and the economics of religion, including Confucianism and Tibetan Buddhism. I have become interested in the tendency of governments to deliberately destroy religions of subjugated peoples, as has occurred in Tibet.

¶15   I hope to teach overseas in the near future while continuing to study different nations—their cultures, histories, and languages. I would like to somehow bring the world closer together, and I believe that I can best do this by gaining expertise in one area and sharing my understanding with others through writing and teaching.

¶16   My proposed project under the fellowship involves cycling from Beijing to Guangzhou to Lhasa. My route passes through the most important religious sites in China, and my mode of travel allows me to interact with people from all over China—not just those of the largest cities, or those who live near tourist attractions. While cycling seems ideal because it would offer maximum exposure to the land and people of China, the same journey could be done by train and bus if necessary due to unexpected changes in Chinese tourism policies. The logistics, contingencies and other details of this trip are covered in Part II of this essay.

ESSAY #11

The following candidate wrote to me, "This essay came in very handy during my interview with the admissions committee. It served as an ice-breaker which set the tone for the rest of the interview. While writing this essay, I kept in mind a couple of important things: I wanted to address all the critical issues (thoughts on family, contribution of spouse, experience relative to medical school, outside achievements/interests which contributed to 'well-roundedness'), and I wanted to explain but make no excuses for previous shortcomings. This was, of course, a very personal essay. I feel that it incorporated a sense of sincerity and devotion to my goals . . . . PS: I might add that the interviewers did not even ask me *why* I wanted to be a physician. They also told me that my dedication, self-motivation, and maturity showed through in the essay; so there was no pressure on me [in the interview] to prove to them that I had these qualities."

AMCAS Essay for Medical School

¶1   Not long ago, a chill went down my spine as the center judge raised my hand in victory, and the crowd roared for me in congratulations and excitement. I had just earned the chance to qualify for the United States Olympic Team in Tae Kwon Do, and I thought that I had achieved the highest possible honor; but, I was mistaken. In May I will graduate from IPFW with highest distinction—an honor which far surpasses all previous ones, especially after such a shaky start in college at ISU.

¶2   My attitude at ISU was nonchalant, and my priorities were obviously shuffled. Even though I was not a serious student there and had no long-term academic goals, my time spent at ISU was meaningful for it was there that I was introduced to martial arts, which has taught me many important things: That desire and determination underlie success in reaching goals, that a person sets his/her own limits—no one sets them for him/her, and that the body and mind are interrelated. Through martial arts and a sincere desire to change, I have become self-disciplined, self-confident, coordinated, and mentally strong. I have also learned how to rechannel negative energies (like anxiety and frustration) into positive action. I have utilized all of these tools to this day at home, work, and school.

¶3   After two years at ISU, I began my own chain of physical fitness and karate schools and continued to compete on a national level. During this three-year period of self-employment, I realized several things about myself which motivated me to consider a career in medicine. I discovered that I interact easily with others—I am "people oriented"—and that I can grasp complicated material and make sense of it. I also came to recognize my need to be challenged and to make a positive difference in the lives of other people. Martial arts prompted a curiosity in me about how the human body works: What are its most vital areas? What can cause these vital areas to malfunction and how can they subsequently be fixed? What is anatomically/chemically involved in movement, pain perception, and the process of healing? It was obvious to me that I had much to learn, and I yearned for a deeper understanding of the mental and physical human processes and the opportunity to direct this knowledge so as to help others in a very real way.

¶4   So I went back to school. This time I went as a devoted student with concrete and realistic goals, and I set out to demonstrate that I had academic potential. In addition to going to school, I have worked as a phlebotomist at Parkview Hospital where I have had extensive patient contact. This job has enhanced my education beyond my classroom lectures. I have become very familiar with all areas of the hospital including ER, oncology, pediatrics, ICU, neonatal, trauma, orthopaedics, and others. Furthermore, I have observed such techniques as CPR, catheterization, EEG, suturing, respiratory therapy, X-ray, EKG, and childbirth, to name a few. I have also become more and more sensitive to the pains that others endure. My experiences as a phlebotomist have helped me to develop a good bedside manner; I have found that the smallest of things—a friendly hello or a pat on the hand to let a patient know that you care—can make a significant difference in how a patient feels and can even affect his/her progress.

¶5   As a physician I can look forward to continuous challenge and a lifetime of learning. I realize that a physician's schedule may interfere with family plans, but I can tolerate these sacrifices with the support of my understanding husband who has been my inspiration—behind me 100% from the beginning. We both consider this to be a family endeavor; we are both in excellent health and prepared to make the required commitment. Becoming a physician will satisfy my need to make a contribution by utilizing my education to help others in need on a daily basis. This, after all, is what life is about; and being able to do this is, truly, the highest possible honor.

ESSAY #12

The theme of this next essay is rather straightforward: "Why I want to become a lawyer." The exposition of that theme, the interplay between the humorous and the mortally serious, is not so straightforward. This essay is a paradigm of the "less is more" principle. Note how much material is covered so briefly. Instead of dragging the reader through every aspect of the campaign trail and her time in Washington, she trusts that they will infer much of the experience.

Personal Statement for Law School

¶1   Even though everyone warns me that it's not going to be "Rage of Angels" or "L.A. Law," I want to go to law school. Despite the thirty-pound textbooks and the long hours, despite the strange vocabulary of torts, procedures, and *Black's Legal Dictionary*, despite the lines at the photocopy machine, I want to go to law school. I ignore the bumper-stickers that read "The last thing our country needs is another lawyer" and that quote from *Henry VI*.

¶2   I want to become a lawyer, even though a record number of people are trying: innumerable heads bent over countless test sheets, with candy, extra pencils, clocks resting nearby on empty seats. Those standardized questions wormed their way into the fabric of my thinking, so that I imagined daily disagreements in a "Facts and Issues" format or saw the difficulty of untangling our apartment's phone bill as a logic problem. (If each roommate called Boston, but only Gretchen called Kansas City, who called Detroit?) And graduates confide that these changes intensify, your thinking becomes fundamentally altered, synapses fire in new and permanent directions, and you become habituated to logic and argument. I met a young law-school couple at the beach. They stood waist-deep in the ocean, holding hands, pushed gently by the water as they discussed rights of privacy. But none of these prospects dissuades me.

¶3   During my year away from school, I worked in Kit Bond's Senate campaign and Washington office. For that entire year, my attention was focussed on aspects of law: those who make the laws, the laws themselves, and the effects they have on the public. During the campaign, my position as deputy director of issues and policy development showed me the unexpected results laws can have, and how even the most well-intentioned decision can hurt a sector of constituents. Later as a legislative correspondent, I prepared texts which clarified issues to constituents and justified our office's position. Often, however, complaints about Senate actions were well-founded. Missourians were hurt by a benignant law which had an unavoidable negative consequence, or by the scrupulous attention to the exact language of a law which worked to subvert, rather than promote, its intent.

¶4   But alongside the unfortunate results, I watched the struggle to create a reasonable and articulate code. I saw drafts of legislation change shape as Congress hammered out the final form of a new law; I studied elegant and cogent Supreme Court decisions which exemplify the beauty of a tightly-worked argument, carefully expressed, from which the law derives its power.

¶5   So I still want to become a lawyer, despite those terrible, ubiquitous jokes, despite that line about liars and lawyers from *sex, lies and videotape,* despite all the cliches. Have you read Oliver Wendell Holmes? "But remotely what the lawyer does is to establish, develop, or illuminate rules which are to govern the conduct of men for centuries; to set in motion principles and influences which shape the thought and action of generations which know not by whose command they move."

¶6   That's why I want to become a lawyer.

ESSAY #13

The next essay is somewhat more formal in tone. Note how in ¶4 the applicant introduces important influences on her area of interest in anthropology. In ¶5 and ¶6 the candidate discusses some details of her proposed methodology. Finally, in ¶7 she mentions her existing rapport with a professor at the targeted school.

Personal Statement for Doctoral Program in Anthropology

¶1   I am applying to the Johns Hopkins graduate program in anthropology because of the specialization of the faculty in the anthropology of health, social inequality, gender, and culture. I have found that an historical look at birth in America presents a useful vehicle to examine how medical knowledge reflects beliefs about the social order, particularly gender roles.

¶2   My first paper on this subject looked at the development of obstetrics in early twentieth-century America. During this period birth was defined as a more dangerous event than it had been previously, giving obstetrics a status in the medical profession that it otherwise would not have held. The paper emphasized the use of specialized knowledge in the establishment of social status, by arguing that the rise in medical intervention during birth was motivated by the obstetricians' conscious intent to improve their professional position. However, some of the material that I came across suggested that women had been the driving force in bringing anesthesia to American delivery rooms. These women saw anesthesia not only as pain relief but also as a form of liberation. In light of the present demand by many women for more "natural" births this earlier campaign presented an intriguing topic for study. I decided to use it as one of the case studies for the independent research paper required for my honors degree. I described the campaign by women for the use of anesthesia in birth and the diagnosis of neurasthenia in nineteenth-century America to show how these debates about medical issues helped to define the relationship between women's social status and reproductive functions. It was important to me to illuminate the participation of the women themselves in this process, and to depict these relationships not as stagnant but as part of a process of change and redefinition.

¶4   Social scientists like John and Barbara Ehrenreich, Andrew Treacher, and Peter Wright take a critical approach to the wider influence of medical knowledge in society. I propose to examine how those outside as well as those inside the medical profession use the body as a metaphor to express their views of the social order.

¶5   I feel that an important aspect of the anthropological approach is that the artifacts of everyday life and common concern are given equal weight to those of figures of authority. In the course of my undergraduate research I found a wealth of material from medical texts of the period. However, I also tried to gain an understanding of the laity's experience through popular literature such as novels and women's magazines. In this way I hoped to communicate the metaphoric equality of medical knowledge and its reflection of the larger culture.

¶6   In anthropological research, using an historical case has a particular fascination, and it offers some advantages for inquiry. The accumulation of evidence over time and, in the case of medical texts, the unguarded testimony of doctors who were less closely scrutinized than they are today are two advantages of this perspective. On the other hand, it is much more difficult to interpret the subjective experience of individuals without being able to pose questions directly or to choose the subjects of the study. The forces of historical selection filter the anthropologist's access to the population. For this reason I would like to do a study of contemporary beliefs about the body into which I could incorporate field work and personal interviews.

¶7   Since graduating from college, I have become more curious about the changes in cultural belief when one system of knowledge such as Western science emerges or ascends over another such as religion. I believe that the rapid advancements of medical technology, the movement of Western medicine into all areas of the world, and the diversity of cultural belief within North America present enormous areas which demand a greater understanding of the cultural implications of the body. I have been corresponding with Prof. Whitney-Wingrove concerning possible topics for further research.

¶8   I hope that Johns Hopkins will consider my academic record and my keen interest in the area so that I may add to this body of research.

ESSAY #14

This essay is a clear and articulate presentation of a minority point of view. Most applicants to this law school will be interested in corporate law, commercial litigation, insurance defense, and other "big money" aspects of the law. Candidates are often hesitant to take minority stands, but this is misguided. Admissions readers repeatedly told me they appreciate a heartfelt presentation of a possibly unpopular position. You can bet that this candidate is going to contribute to the educational process of the other, more traditional students, and admissions directors are quite aware of this.

Statement of Purpose for Law School

¶1   My decision to apply to law school stems directly from my career as a union representative. Throughout my life I have been committed to political activism and social change, and law school is the next logical step.

¶2   I first became involved in politics before college, when I worked for State and U.S. Representatives (see c.v.). These experiences lent me insight into the political process, but they frustrated my need to advocate for people I felt were underprivileged and unfairly treated.

¶3   During my college summers I worked on and studied an Israeli kibbutz where I saw firsthand that an industry could function profitably while workers are treated as equals. In this country, labor unions are still the premier vehicle by which employees strive for fair treatment.

¶4   Since graduation I have worked with the Service Employees International Union (SEIU). While the labor movement suffered serious losses since the 1980s, SEIU has been growing tremendously, becoming the fifth largest union in the AFL-CIO. Over the past seven years, I have directed many successful organizing drives, culminating in several thousand new members. This fall, I was promoted to affiliation coordinator, responsible for drawing the 100,000-member California School Employees Association into the SEIU—a move that will boost our membership by 15 percent. More importantly, the increase will allow working people in the schools to have a greater voice in the statewide and national agenda for educational reform.

¶5   In addition to organizing, I have negotiated dozens of labor-management contracts. I led bargaining teams that confronted management with members' demands. In protracted sessions, I would sit across from veteran attorneys and hammer out agreements. On every occasion, I won better wages, benefits, and contract language for my members. I persistently defended these gains in grievance arbitrations. Ultimately, my supervisor appointed me the union's chief advocate for disciplinary appeals.

¶6   A law degree would enable me to undertake new challenges. As a labor lawyer, I could continue my representation of union members but on a grander scale. Labor boards and courts render decisions that overwhelmingly impact the scope of a union's activity, often determining its very existence. In Congress, bar associations, and the union's top echelons, attorneys are drafting workplace legislation that could redefine labor-management relations: these laws would stop unfair job terminations, prohibit closing plants without notice, and allow employees greater prospects for joint ownership of their companies. I am enthusiastic about taking part in these legal challenges and opportunities.

¶7   I plan to be an outstanding law student. My tenure in the labor movement has equipped me with verbal and advocacy skills and exposed me to the law from a nonacademic perspective. I originally took the LSATs senior year at Harvard and my 99th percentile score reflects my aptitude when steeped in academia.

¶8   Hastings is one of two law schools to which I am applying. Because I presently work only one block away, I am familiar with the campus and the many valuable services it offers such as the workers' rights clinic, speaker series, and law library. I am particularly impressed with its labor law professors, its academic challenge, and the law journal. I hope I am offered the opportunity to study at Hastings.

ESSAY #15

Medical schools are admitting more students with non-premed backgrounds than ever before. Although you must take the science prerequisites for medical school, you need not major in biology, chemistry, microbiology, or other traditional premedical areas of study. This is more fully addressed in Zebala and Jones' book, *Medical School Admissions: The Insider's Guide.*

AMCAS Essay for Medical School

¶1   Thoughts about AIDS, and the treatment of people with AIDS, helped me to determine my choice of a topic for my senior thesis in history. I decided to study the relationship of medicine to the morals of the society in which it is practiced. Specifically, I chose to research and write about the treatment of patients with venereal disease in nineteenth-century America. Rummaging through medical textbooks, journal articles, and popular treatises of the last century, I was impressed by the parallels between then and now. AIDS, like syphilis and gonorrhea in the 1800s, has not been treated as just a disease, but also as a 'scarlet letter,' as evidence of deviant behavior and moral wrongdoing. A hundred years ago, physicians were trained to be the guardians of sexual morality, and to give a dose of condemnation with every prescribed regimen of mercury vapors. Now, supposedly, health care providers learn to deliver nondiscriminatory treatment, based on knowledge of physiology and pathogenesis, rather than on notions of sin and retribution. The extent to which modern medicine falls short of this paradigm was clearly illustrated by the response of the medical community to AIDS. It has become evident that medicine is not all scientific objectivity, and that health care is still strongly influenced by personal and societal concepts of right and wrong. This understanding of how closely linked medicine is to the values of its practitioners will guide me in my own work. I hope that it will help me to recognize times when biases and fears are adversely affecting my interactions and decisions. I hope that it will enable me to educate without condemning, and to care for people without blaming them, implicitly or directly, for their ailments.

¶2   When I graduated, I wanted to involve myself further with science. I found a job in a lab which studies HIV and other retroviruses. Here I have learned the basic grammar of molecular biology. I have gained vocabulary and knowledge which will help me all my life to understand developments in AIDS research and other fields. I have learned some about the process of science, about how experiments do not necessarily yield answers, but many other questions, and about how one shapes a project by choosing which of these to pursue, which to postpone, and which to abandon altogether. In the lab, HIV is a genome, a set of regulatory proteins, a fascinating puzzle, and a challenge. Though I love what I am doing, I feel somewhat distanced from the social and clinical realities of AIDS. I am anxious to begin learning the clinical side of medical science now, to begin training for a position in which I can translate idea into practice, intent into action.

¶3   My generation is the first to have grown up in an age which is practically free from tuberculosis and polio, in a time when medicine has been nearly invincible in the battle against contagious diseases. The AIDS epidemic has renewed fears and doubts which have been at rest for many years.

¶4   We will need to learn the value of providing comfort and relief from pain even when there is no hope for recovery or cure. From the knowledge and the insights which I have gathered in my studies and in my work, I have created a vision of the physician I would like to become.

ESSAY #16

The student who wrote this next essay told me she thought she came across to the admissions counselors as "that crazy radio lady." She said she earned an interview with this essay, and she won over the committee with her sense of purpose to an unusual goal. Once again, admissions counselors are drawn to people who they think will succeed *whether they are admitted or not.* This candidate certainly leaves that impression.

Statement of Purpose for Graduate School of Business

¶1   Radio has been my passion for as long as I can remember. I was one of those high school kids who sat by the radio waiting for the magic touch tones to dial in and win; my fascination with the medium was kindled.

¶2   My college radio station, WXXX at [major university], actually let me on the air. I'd get up for my 3 a.m. shift to play the Dead Kennedys to insomniacs in the greater metro area. An internship at a 'real world' station substituted for my senior thesis, and launched me into professional radio.

¶3   In the seven plus years that I've been out in the working world, my objective has not changed: I want to own my own radio station. Maybe a station group, even a network.

¶4   I often try to analyze what it is about this medium that excites me so much. The immediacy of it. The power to reach people, relay a message, get under people's skins. As a work environment, I adore the wacky people attracted to radio. The casual type of workplace. The fact that a station is a small business where creativity can flourish, and one person can make an impact. And as an institution, a radio station can and should be an integral part of its community. Its voice, its friend.

¶5   And despite all the predictions to the contrary, radio is still alive and well. Prices of stations remain sky-high. Radio is omnipresent. As an industry, there is a lot of action—more and more stations are becoming increasingly specialized—all-talk, all-sports, all Elvis? Is AM stereo going to get off the ground? Will the new administration change the joint ownership laws? What is the future of AM radio as young people grow up listening only to FM? There are so many questions, and in my mind, a lot of opportunity for bold thinkers—who have the knowledge to make their ideas into reality.

¶6   Recently I made a decisive move toward attaining my goal. I became an account executive for a major market station. I knew that unless I could effectively sell radio, I'd never be able to successfully run a station. Sales is the traditional route to advancement in radio: good salespeople become sales managers who become general managers. I know that if I stick with it, I can rise to the top via this route.

¶7   The truth is, I've worked for a good number of general managers who rose through the ranks through the sales department, and frankly, I am not impressed.

¶8   This business requires more knowledge than one can acquire by simply climbing the sales ladder. I need to know accounting and finance. If I don't know how to put together a deal, who's going to bankroll my first acquisition? With an increasingly media-intensive market, how can I strategically position my station to garner its share of the ad dollars? With all the diverse personalities and egos in a 'showbiz' enterprise like a radio station, being a good people manager is essential, but so is knowing how to utilize resources and how to streamline an organization. These are just a few of my goals for business school.

¶9   I am very impressed by Columbia's diverse offerings in all these areas. I will learn the entrepreneurial skills I need, while having the opportunity to interact with leaders and top students, with interests both similar and diverse from my own. I hope to take advantage of some of the Graduate School of Journalism's offerings as well. And by staying in New York City, I hope to keep up with my valuable contacts, developed in my years already in this business.

ESSAY #17

Can you imagine how many homemade VHS video shorts the admissions office at UCLA's Film School reviews every year? This candidate uses physics and computer science to put a spin on his application. Note that he has made a key contact at the school already, as mentioned in ¶6.

Statement of Purpose for Film School

¶1   As animation and technology transform, it is my objective to continue molding technology into a versatile tool that expands the animator's creative potential.

¶2   The foundations of my skills in computers were built while I was a physics student at Reed College, a science institute masquerading as a liberal arts college. The computer systems I designed to graphically display planetary motion, projectile motion, and fluid dynamics gave me a visual reference which proved to be essential to understanding the mathematical equations that describe these phenomena. The effectiveness with which computer graphics communicates physical concepts motivated me to use computers for my senior thesis in image processing and character recognition. My thesis (see c.v.) culminated in the creation of a computer system which scanned images and produced three-dimensional graphs of their spatial harmonics.

¶3   My use of computer graphics as a means of understanding scientific phenomena continued after graduation when I earned a summer fellowship at the Neurological Sciences Institute. My work there focused on the effect of moving images on human balance (see c.v.). The research team had trouble isolating the motion of the subject's visual plane while the subject moved. To aid our understanding I created an application which used the motion of the subject's joints to calculate the displacement of her visual plane. As the stick figure moved according to the displacement of the joint angles, the other images would display the resultant displacement of the figure's visual plane.

¶4   In order to broaden my knowledge of computers I began pursuing a career as a consultant in the design and development of information processing systems. In the past two years I have had the opportunity to hone my skills in a number of different areas in computer systems design (see c.v.). It is necessary in my work as a computer consultant to quickly adapt to new technology. In fact my adaptability is the most versatile skill I have acquired as a consultant. I am undaunted by technological innovation, and strive to master it as rapidly as possible. Now, instead of adapting to advances in technology, I want to initiate those advancements and have my motivation be the desire to produce animation.

¶5   Animation fascinates me because it combines the visual arts and motion. My initial appreciation of the visual arts was due to my father, who was an accomplished illustrator, animator, and layout artist. Physics added to that appreciation by developing my understanding of geometry and spatial relations. My interest in motion stems from my study of the dynamics of motion in physics and my experience in ballet and jazz dance. In physics I learned how things move and why, and in dance I became aware of the emotional impact that dynamic gestures convey.

¶6   I want to return to school to plunge into an artistically creative environment where I can both develop my sense of visual aesthetics and apply my computer skills to animation. An environment which is strong in both aesthetics and technology is unusual, and my discussions with Phil Mittelman have led me to believe that this rare environment is at UCLA.

ESSAY #18

This next essay is thematic in construction. Note that one issue the candidate builds her essay on, the zoning struggle outlined in ¶4-6, *she was not directly involved in.* This is risky. Several admissions counselors told me they preferred essays not include struggles or issues to which the candidate was not a direct party. However, this author succeeds in weaving this story into the overall presentation of her political philosophy. It is a rather compelling presentation, and she earned admission to every program to which she applied.

Personal Statement for Master in Public Policy Program

¶1   When I think of my roots I see Cameron House, the Chinatown community center on the corner of Joice and Sacramento in San Francisco. Joice is not a street; it is an alley. For many Chinese-American youths, it is an alley of fellowship, leadership, camping skills, and summer fun. For new immigrants, it is an alley of safety and English tutoring. For battered women it is an alley of refuge and counseling. Joice alley is an exciting place of learning and caring because the people at Cameron House are committed to serving the Asian-American community.

¶2   Growing up at Cameron House, I learned leadership, communication, and group cooperation skills. Not only did I learn silly camp songs, but I learned how to pass those songs on to others. In thirteen years, I went from day camp camper to day camp director. At the University of California at Santa Cruz (U.C. Santa Cruz), these skills were essential to the success of my academic and extra-curricular work. I incorporated my listening and communication skills as a selected undergraduate teaching assistant for an American studies survey course. The Asian-American anthology which I co-edited embodied group vision, dedication, discussion, and compromise. As an English conversation teacher in Japan, I found patience, encouragement, and laughter my most effective teaching tools. Most importantly, Cameron House has taught me that I have responsibility for more than just myself; I have responsibility to others.

¶3   I majored in American studies because I found its interdisciplinary analysis creative and useful. By integrating knowledge, American studies trained me to make connections and to see the world in its totality instead of in the compartmentalized world of a single academic discipline. For example, I used American studies tools in my Citizenship class where I co-wrote a paper entitled "Watsonville Redistricting:

Redefining Power." This paper examined the recent political transformations in the small agricultural town near my university. In Watsonville, like in many California and Texas cities with large Hispanic populations, there is underrepresentation of Latinos in political offices. My colleague and I were interested in placing the redistricting of Watsonville court case in a larger economic, political, and social context. As a result, we looked at factors like migrating labor patterns, organized labor unions, language discrimination, established family networks, and "company town" infrastructures. This analysis demonstrated that underrepresentation was not an accident but a result of the at-large electoral process. The variety of academic tools I have developed are personally meaningful when I can take them back to Chinatown.

¶4   For example, as a child, I was always puzzled by the large, vacant lot across from Cameron House. Over the years it went from a make-shift garbage dump to an alternative playground, and then into a temporary shelter from the rain. Now, this lot is Mei Lun Yuen, a 500-resident home for low-income families and the elderly. Because I was not looking for connections, the transformation appeared accidental to me, a kind of metropolistic evolution.

¶5   Metropolistic evolution, however, does not recognize political processes, condominium interests, or community resistance. The Mei Lun Yuen housing unit symbolizes the crucial public policy issue of land use. Over twenty years ago, the one-acre lot was controversial land because it sat squarely on the border between Chinatown and gentrified, upper-class Nob Hill. The Chinatown community wanted the vacant land for much needed low-income housing, but the Nob Hill residents organized and fought the plan arguing that the project would obstruct their views, lower their property values, and bring in crime, filth, and overcrowding.

¶6   While the Nob Hill Neighbors hired lawyers to represent their interests, the Chinatown Coalition for Better Housing countered with pickets, protests, letter writing, pressure at the mayor's office, and packing the city's redevelopment hearings. From 1970 to 1980, there were four different presidential administration changes—when the rules change in Washington, they change for Chinatown. The Chinatown Coalition became well versed in the political process. After spending over a quarter of a million dollars on legal fees, finally the Nob Hill Neighbors gave up on the drawn out struggle and Mei Lun Yuen was built. For me it is exciting to know that when a community joins the public policy process, it can successfully shape its own future.

¶7   This summer, I studied at the University of Washington as a Ford Fellow (previously the Sloan Fellowship program) in the Minority Advancement Program (MAP). I enjoyed the summer institute because the case study method challenged me to integrate economic, computer, writing, statistical, and negotiating skills. The most exciting and meaningful part of the program was when we, the MAP fellows, made public policy personal and connected it back to our own histories and communities. A remote politics, when brought into our communities, became an intimate politics. This intimacy generated new questions. What does public policy have to say about immigrant Vietnamese youth and the educational system? How can computers empower the African-American community of Chicago? Where can the Chicano community put pressure to halt the spraying of dangerous pesticides in the farmer's fields where many of their members work? These are the kind of questions that need to be asked and need to be answered.

¶8   I would like to pursue a masters of public policy degree at the John F. Kennedy School of Government at Harvard University because it leads to a career in which I can actively use my skills and sensibilities, and which allows me to do what I care about. I am most excited about courses on aging and women and public policy. With my roots at Joice and Sacramento, and my education at U.C. Santa Cruz, I am committed to making the connections. I want to be someone who involves the people into the political process, linking the Capitol to the alleys of Chinatown, the city council to the lettuce fields, and the redevelopment agencies to forgotten neighborhoods. To me, this is good public policy.

ESSAY #19

Like essays #11 and #15, this is an AMCAS essay for medical school. The AMCAS form has a prescribed box into which the admissions essay must fit, and it is important to note that no letters of recommendation or supporting materials of any kind are allowed. This makes the admission essay extremely important. If schools are interested in the candidate, they will request additional materials, known as secondaries. In this AMCAS essay, note the straightforward coverage of the candidate's grades in her first undergraduate career, ¶1-2. If you are not admitted to medical school on your first round, you should note that many students are admitted after strengthening their backgrounds as this candidate did. Also note the proper use of working titles in ¶4 and ¶8 for research in process.

AMCAS Essay for Medical School

¶1 When I was an undergraduate at the University of California, Davis, I wanted to be a physician. Although I always excelled in the life sciences, I had to work 20 to 32 hours per week throughout my first years of college, and I graduated without honors status (B.S., Human Biology, a pre-medicine major I designed in collaboration with the faculty).

¶2 I was very dissatisfied with this performance, as I was sure I could have excelled had I had more time for my studies. I re-affirmed my commitment to healthcare as a career, and I studied nursing at the University of California, Los Angeles. There I applied myself and graduated *magna cum laude* (B.S., Nursing).

¶3 I then pursued a nursing career with zeal, selecting a path that would allow me to stress medicine, autonomy, and decision-making in my work. After serving a year on a medical-surgical floor, I accepted a position with the Kidney Transplant Unit (KTU) at the University of California, San Francisco, Medical Center (UCSF Medical Center). This position allowed me to gain in-depth knowledge of a specific patient population, and gave me opportunities to advance my assessment skills. My nursing skill was acknowledged in formal and informal ways, including my nomination for the Sophie Robinson Award for excellence in nursing, and I served on many in-service and quality assurance committees.

¶4 Next I was selected for the position of physician extender for the Renal Transplant Service at UCSF Medical Center, where I was hired by the Department of Surgery to assist house staff in meeting patient needs. I attended twice daily rounds, followed up on radiographic, laboratory and consult reports, performed routine house staff procedures, and occasionally assisted in OR. This was a custom-designed nursing position, and I was allowed to define the role to the extent that I oriented and worked side-by-side with interns. I was also invited to serve as research assistant, collecting data on drug side effects under direction of Juliet Melzer, M.D., UCSF Medical Center, on a project with the working title of "Investigational drug study on MALG (Minnesota Anti-Lymphocyte Globulin)."

¶5   After 18 months of this experience, which I enjoyed thoroughly, I decided to obtain critical care experience and began to apply for competitive positions in this area. I obtained an appointment to the Cornell University Medical Center at New York Hospital as a post-anesthesia care nurse. In this position I provided post-op care for cardiac, neurologic, pediatric, trauma, burn, and vascular patients. This was exciting work, with a diverse patient population. This is also when I decided once again to become a physician. Because of the following event, I realized that the intellectual challenges of nursing were no longer enough for me, and I made my decision to go on to medical school and become a physician.

¶6   I received a 42-year-old female with a newly placed peritoneal shunt. (She had had an 11-year history of ovarian cancer, and a chronic ascites problem requiring frequent paracentesis.) She awoke combative, and was quickly extubated by the anesthesiologist. Her recovery deteriorated, as she developed pulmonary edema, a temperature of 40 degrees centigrade, and right-sided heart failure. I provided the critical direct nursing care to this patient for hours while the interns consulted on approaches to her treatment. I was acutely aware that my abilities and knowledge were limited to nursing, and I very much wanted to be able to contribute meaningfully to the intellectual debate I was witnessing among the interns.

¶7   The attending physician was summoned to survey the problem. He clamped the shunt and put her on antibiotics, recognizing that the patient's heart was not strong enough to handle the large fluid load. The patient went to ICU, and I decided to go to medical school.

¶8   I returned to the Kidney Transplant Unit of UCSF Medical Center and began to study for the MCATs. Also, I took a course in hematology from San Francisco State University, and served as a research assistant on two additional projects: (1) I conducted GFR studies as an assistant to Nephrology Research Fellow, Carlos Stempl, M.D., UCSF Medical Center, on a project with a working title, "Does Verapamil improve GFR in transplant recipients?" and (2) I am currently research assistant under the direction of William Amend, M.D., UCSF Medical Center, performing the retrospective arm of a two-armed study, "Incidence of Cytomegalovirus in transplant patients and the efficacy of Acyclovir prophylaxis."

¶9   My ultimate career direction is to practice infectious disease medicine. Witnessing the devastation these organisms can cause on immunocompromised patients has given me a great appreciation for the role of the physician, to intercede and reverse the course of infectious disease. I would find this work immensely interesting and rewarding, and I look forward to the opportunity to pursue it.

¶10   With more than enough energy and stamina to succeed, I am intellectually, emotionally, and financially prepared for medical school. I will admit no more impediments to my goal. I am eager to begin the process.

ESSAY #20

This candidate is clearly going to be an asset to any department he might join. He has articulated his reasons for selecting a school stronger in archeology than in marine archeology, ¶2, and it would seem that any school would be interested in his affiliation with Oxford's M.A.R.E. This is another example of a student who is going to excel whether he is admitted to any particular program or not.

Personal Statement for Doctoral Program in Anthropology (Archaeology)

¶1   The peculiar fact that archaeology is both a social and physical science forms the basis of my attraction to the study. The process whereby information gained from chemistry and geology is transformed into statements about human culture and society fascinates me. I have chosen to study archaeology because it is one of the few fields I have found which demands a knowledge of metallurgy in order to make statements about trade networks, or of religious forms to understand settlement patterning—in short, an open and enquiring mind into all aspects of the past and present world as a basis for an understanding of humankind. I am applying to Brown University because my investigations have led me to believe that I will find an atmosphere of intellectual interest and diversity in faculty, students, and course work paralleling those I would like to see in myself.

¶2   An overworked catechism among marine archaeologists is that "there is no such thing as marine archaeology, only archaeology under water," but after four years of exposure to the field I am skeptical. The dichotomy in archaeology between technique and technology on the one hand, and the questions of human social processes which these try to answer, is not fully appreciated by many. My experiences on projects in Jamaica, Bermuda, and Italy, and my personal research into the matter, has led me to believe that technique exists in marine archaeology apart from any humanistic component, and that most researchers follow the Gary Cooper school of "shoot first, ask questions later." Even after thirty years, most of its intellectual parameters continue to be defined not by the archaeologists, but by the artifacts themselves. Although there is no doubt that other institutions in the United States and abroad offer fine education in the techniques of marine archaeology, techniques, in and of themselves, hold little interest for me. These techniques should only be a means, and my studies at Brown will be directed towards understanding and defining an end.

¶3   In general, therefore, what I would like to do while at Brown is to examine the nature of the interaction between human social processes and the maritime environment and to see what light marine archaeology can throw on existing questions of human culture change. On a more specific level I am currently interested in the following questions: Did the deforestation of Crete lead to the decline of the Minoan civilization as a sea-power; was the site of Troy an inevitability given the nature of the Hellespont and the abilities of Bronze age shipping; and at what point in time, if at all, were the Myceneans able to penetrate the Black Sea to the Danube, perhaps for tin from Bohemia?

¶4   Given the nature of these questions it seems logical that I should stay at Oxford. My professors are pleased with my work to date and have asked me to stay on to complete a D.Phil. There are two reasons for which I have chosen to apply to Brown instead of staying on. On a pragmatic level I have financed my year here without any financial aid by working for two years; I am unwilling to spend the equivalent of a small condominium or two BMWs for three more years. Money aside, I enjoy teaching and intend to make a career of it at the university level. Oxford does not emphasize teaching for its graduate students, and I feel that an important part of my education is lacking. Although I will be leaving Oxford I will maintain my ties here and I expect that my involvement with M.A.R.E. (the marine archaeological research expedition) will continue, allowing both myself, and hopefully other students at Brown, an opportunity to do marine archaeology in the Mediterranean.

¶5   In conclusion, I would like to say that given my interests and concerns, I feel Brown is the very best place for me to be. The facilities, scholarship, and traditions of the institution, combined with the calibre of the student body, make me confident that I will be stimulated throughout the course of my studies. I feel confident of my ability to succeed and hope that I have demonstrated a commitment to, and some ability in, the study of archaeology.

ESSAY #21

Many people think that once a student gets into medical school her career is set for life. Not so. Medical doctors compete vigorously for a seemingly unending series of internships, residencies, fellowships, and programs of advanced training. This candidate used this essay as part of a successful application for a residency in otolaryngology, at fifty-to-one odds.

Personal Statement for Residency in Otolaryngology

¶1   Otolaryngology attracted me for three main reasons. First, my father recently retired as Director of the Boston Center for Hearing and Speech. Through his involvement in speech pathology and audiology, I've been exposed to some aspects of otolaryngology all my life. Second, I'm interested in the opportunity to practice with all ages of patients, from children to the elderly. Third, I am drawn by the combination of medical and surgical practice.

¶2   I've done very well in school, both as an undergraduate at M.I.T. and as a medical student at [name withheld]. Last year I was awarded one of the two Lange Book awards for outstanding scholastic achievement. I also have significant undergraduate awards for scholarship.

¶3   Research is an aspect of graduate medical training for which I have both an interest and a sound background. This summer I was a research assistant to Drs. S. McQuown and T.A. Cook: effects of liposuction on porcine fat cell populations. While at M.I.T. I learned well the investigative thinking of basic research with extensive experience in biochemistry, cell biology, and histology. During my last year I completed a senior honors thesis involving the laboratory investigation of protein-folding mechanisms: *Deamidation of Glutamine and Asparagine Residues: An Approach to the Study of Protein Folding*

¶4   I find working with my hands quite satisfying. For the last seven years I have supported myself in part by cleaning and repairing microscopes at colleges, universities, and research centers throughout the greater metropolitan area. During my surgical rotation at Good Samaritan Hospital, I was encouraged by two of the attending surgeons, who remarked that I showed surprising facility for surgery for one so early in a medical career (see letters of recommendation).

¶5   In addition to these technical and academic facilities, I am able to interact with and enjoy a great spectrum of people; this is one of my strongest personality traits.

¶6   On the personal side, my wife Heather and I have been married for two years and have future plans for children. She is attending university for a teaching degree and will graduate next spring.

¶7   I believe I have the skills (academic, social, and manual), and the interest to excel in the field of otolaryngology. The time ahead of me will be exciting. I look forward to the discovery and the challenge of my chosen career.

ESSAY #22

The Rhodes scholarship is reserved for those students who demonstrate excellence in a combination of academics, community service, and sports. This essayist does not mention his participation in sports, but you can be assured that somewhere else in his application he makes ample mention of his accomplishments in this area. The quite frequent use of great writers and thinkers in this essay is effective only because the writer has such a firm grasp on their works.

Application Essay for Rhodes Scholarship

¶1   In Plato's *Protagoras,* Socrates begins his interrogation of Hippocrates with the question: "What will you become?" Socrates repeats this question with increasing fury as he rebukes Hippocrates for planning to become wise by listening to the sophist Protagoras. Socrates does not care that Hippocrates will waste money on a few lectures, but instead that he will "risk his greatest treasure" by entrusting the training of his soul to a teacher skilled in speaking rather than in wisdom. Socrates's breathtaking vision of the human potential at stake in education has inspired my commitment to work in public education as well as politics. My study of philosophy began with the Greeks, and I since have found no other thinkers who so profoundly struggle with the issues of education, politics, and their relation to human potential. As I struggle with what I will become, I think the most valuable training would be an intense engagement with the texts of Plato and Aristotle in the classics program at Oxford.

¶2   When I began studying philosophy, I was shocked at Plato's devastating critique of competitive debating, the activity which had dominated my experience through high school. In the *Republic,* Plato argues that such debate suffocates constructive dialogue because it aims at conquest rather than truth. Socrates's final description of the just individual as one who would "participate in the political affairs of the ideal city but not any other [city]" forced me to reassess not only my past debating but my political aspirations.

¶3   With Socrates's words in mind, I avoided the debates of the political organizations on campus, and during my sophomore year I became a tutor for a student struggling with English at Hillhouse High School. After a semester, I guest-taught poetry to a class of inner-city students. We discussed the poem "Dream Deferred," in which Langston Hughes compares a languishing dream to a raisin which dries in the sun. At the end of the class, I asked whether the poem would have been different if Hughes had chosen a plum rather than a raisin. "It would be completely different," a student answered, "because if a raisin dries up, there's nothing, but if a plum dries up, there's a seed; there's hope."

¶4   That answer nourished new dreams, and I decided to teach English in a summer program for economically disadvantaged New Haven students. After the first day of class, I was disheartened because my tenth-grade students angrily resisted reading the *Iliad* on the grounds that it had no relation to their lives as African-Americans. I first tried to argue that Homer was worth reading, which only caused more resentment. When I told my fellow teachers about the problem, many urged me to use stricter discipline to quiet the students' complaints and to proceed with the *Iliad.* But my recent study of Rousseau had convinced me that the excitement I wanted the students to experience could only occur in an atmosphere of freedom. The problem was not only the students' lack of discipline, but the failure of my efforts to respond to their difficulties in reading and enjoying the text. I found that by reading aloud diverse scenes from the *Iliad,* the students could more readily experience the variety of life Homer describes. One student was so moved by his own reading of Hector's farewell to his wife and child that he later wrote an essay which retold the *Iliad* from Hector's perspective. Another student, who initially felt the most oppressed by the class, decided that "Achilles was cool" and wrote in his evaluation: "This was my favorite class because I felt I had some freedom."

¶5   While Rousseau's ideas on education influenced how I taught, his political thought influenced how I responded to the community at Yale. His vision of an active citizenry which contributes to a common goal offered an alternative to the fragmented community I saw outside of class. The challenge remained of how to organize students with diverse interests to contribute to the public good.

¶6   At the beginning of my junior year, I started the Branch program, which organized Yale students to share their interests with public high school students. By the end of that year, one hundred and fifty Yale students were working together with students at Hillhouse High School in programs such as art, drama, writing, recycling, and journalism. Yale students who had earlier passed by more general community service posters found a particular excitement in sharing their enthusiasms for what they loved to do. This enthusiasm was often cut short however, when Hillhouse students did not show up for their appointed meetings. The problems of the inner city can undermine the program by suffocating the high school students' sense of responsibility and their hope. This year Branch has restructured its programs to make them sufficiently reliable and engaging to encourage students to deepen their commitments and their aspirations.

¶7   As I try to respond to problems which can seem overwhelming, I often draw on the philosophy of Immanuel Kant. Kant's conviction that there are no absolute limits on our freedom to change ourselves or others provides grounds for hope. His categorical imperative challenges us to consider ourselves as architects who build a world when we act. Kant's ambitious model of our shared duty to build our society provides a foundation for Rousseau's conception of the active citizen. In my senior thesis, I will continue to explore what I see as the potentially revolutionary power of Kant's vision to respond to the inequalities that ravage our society.

¶8   Kant's vision, however, raises many questions that have urged me to return to a study of the Greeks. Plato and Aristotle's discussion of education and politics would deeply enrich my understanding of what might be done to enable people to realize their freedom. Since Oxford's B.A. program in classics is known for integrating a close study of ancient and modern philosophical texts, there would be no more exciting place to explore the relationship between ancient thought and Kant's philosophy.

¶9   Socrates's question—"what will you become?"—expresses a combination of urgency and hope that underlies my view of politics and education. I share his fury at the reckless devastation of human potential, and also his hope that we can build what we will become. In pursuit of that hope, I plan first to teach in public high school and then to work on local education policy. By the end of my course of study at Oxford, I hope to understand more fully what is at stake in Socrates's question, and be better prepared to respond to it.

ESSAY #23

This is an example of a highly technical essay detailing research projects in chemistry. The reader will be a specialist in this area of chemistry. Note the total lack of personal information.

Research Summary in Application to Doctoral Program in Chemistry

¶1 My first research project involved determining whether the enzyme Uridylate Synthase "channels" the intermediate Orotidine 5'-monophosphate. This is a multifunctional enzyme and explanations for the evolution of this multifunctionality have been somewhat widespread throughout the literature. This project then questioned the basis of these explanations and offered new hypotheses as to why such multifunctional proteins have evolved. I wrote the computer modelling programs which integrated, through recursion, all of the relevant Michaelis-Menton rate equations. This analysis proved that a channelling argument was unnecessary to explain the available experimental evidence. I also performed some related enzyme assays in order to check several related hypotheses developed by Dr. McClard and myself.

¶2 Last summer I worked on an organic synthesis project which involved synthesis of one interesting analogue of a potent, possibly the most potent, regulator of the gluconeogenesis glycolysis pathways fructose 2,5-bisphosphate. The key to the synthesis of the analogue shown below is control of the stereochemistry of the previously anomeric carbon. My work was involved in the reactions with I_2 and Br_2 and creation of the "halogenonium" ion of the Wittig product from the starting protected arabinofructoside sugar, also shown below.

¶3   My current research project, my senior thesis, is related to the one I was involved in during the summer. In this case I am attempting to synthesize an analogue of phosphoribosylpyrophosphate (PRPP) which is the molecule which provides the sugar portion in the *de novo* pathway of pyrimidine biosynthesis. This work utilizes the same synthetic scheme as shown above with the exception of starting with the ribose sugar and several changes in the phosphorous portion of the molecule. The synthetic scheme below shows the route I hope to exploit in synthesizing the target molecule. These projects were all carried out with Prof. McClard at Reed College.

ESSAY #24

Although the title for this postdoctoral essay, as requested on the application form, is "Personal Statement," there is not a shred of personal information in it. The essay contains a proposal for formulation of a chemistry lab and research project, and mentions several prominent chemists who support the proposal. This type of application entails a whole lobbying campaign and extensive personal contact in support of the project, and this essay needs to be considered in that larger context. The ability to make and utilize personal contacts becomes ever more important as your academic career advances.

Personal Statement for National Science Foundation
Postdoctoral Research Fellowship in Chemistry

¶1   The training conducted under this grant would be geared toward establishing a new academic laboratory in which biological, chemical, and physical techniques are focussed on elucidating the fundamental forces and principles of bioorganic and bioinorganic catalytic mechanisms. The strategy of this laboratory would be to elucidate chemical structure/reactivity properties of enzymes and enzyme-bound intermediates leading to the design of experiments which test the nature of transition state stabilization for a given reaction. As chemical systems, some proteins provide excellent, surprisingly tolerant, structurally definable scaffolds for holding probes of the ground states and transition states of catalyzed reactions. Mutant proteins are truly chemical analogues of the wild type structure, and genetics provides an excellent way to generate and test a large number of these analogues (10^8 structures, which would result from randomizing seven amino acid positions, could reasonably be tested genetically). X-ray crystallography and NMR spectroscopy provide powerful, essential, yet incomplete characterization of enzyme chemistry. Fruitful interpretation of good structures can be limited by a paucity of functional information. Therefore, the proposed laboratory would be primarily responsible for generating functional information through the preparation of enzymes, random and site-directed mutant enzymes, inhibitors, and chemically and isotopically modified substrates and cofactors, and through the characterization of the chemical reactions of these reagents. Characterization of the reactions would routinely include genetic function, reaction product analysis, kinetics, and at a minimum, the preparation of suitable samples for x-ray crystallography, NMR spectroscopy, and any other informative techniques. How far the work of the lab extends into the physically oriented techniques will be determined by the extent of the training I am able to accomplish as well as by personnel in the lab; however, collaborations with specialists in crystallographic or spectroscopic techniques will always be preferable to provide as many perspectives on a given project as possible. To the extent that good, effective mathematical models are available, they will be highly considered during the interpretation of results and tested by the design of experiments; e.g., the computer program Del Phi has proven itself a useful model for electrostatic forces in proteins. The laboratory would study many different enzymes with different chemistries at various stages of development. The study of established enzyme systems would provide the most rigorous testing-ground for our knowledge of enzymatic chemistry. The analysis of enzymes with undefined mechanisms would include therapeutic targets where much may be presumed about the chemistry of the enzyme, but where satisfactory, functional inhibitors are still wanted. The social *raison d'être* for this laboratory would be the development of new therapeutic inhibitors based upon the chemistry derived from pursing an understanding of catalysis. The study of enzymes with unknown mechanisms should provide fertile ground for the discovery of new chemistry.

¶2   The proposed postdoctoral work provides an excellent opportunity to establish a project which has much in common with the future work of the proposed laboratory. The enzyme is a therapeutic target with an unknown mechanism. The project hinges on the synthesis of substrate analogues as inhibitors and involves chemical and kinetic characterization of the inhibition, aspects of enzymology in which I am not well trained. In addition, chemical characterization may involve the preparation and analysis of protein crystals.

¶3   The proposed scientific advisor, Prof. Robert Abeles, has established a laboratory where compounds are routinely designed and synthesized with the intent of testing bioorganic and bioinorganic enzymatic mechanisms. As a consequence he provides expertise in an environment where the results of such experiments are routinely analyzed and interpreted. He actively seeks to train his postdoctoral fellows in science while teaching chemistry as it pertains to the analysis of enzyme mechanisms. In short, he operates a laboratory with the focus with which I would like to operate my own. His recommendation would indicate my suitability as the director of such a laboratory.

¶4   Brandeis University presents an excellent faculty. In addition to Dr. Abeles, the biochemistry faculty includes Dr. W. P. Jencks, who is also a particularly lucid and careful chemist and enzymologist. As a sign of the continuing support of penetrating enzymology, the university has recently added to the factory two noted crystallographers, Drs. G. A. Petsko and D. Ringe, whose collaboration with Dr. Abeles is very strong. Their crystallographic program now includes the Laue diffraction technique which allows structural characterization of enzymatic reactions on a millisecond time scale.

CHAPTER 7

LETTERS OF RECOMMENDATION

Your grades, your test scores, your essay, and your letters of recommendation make up the entire weight of evidence the admissions committee has upon which to make its admissions decision. As I hope you have come to realize, different admissions counselors will weigh these factors differently, but no matter how you look at them, letters of recommendation are one of only four sources of information about you, and thus are vitally important.

If you are in any way a borderline candidate, then letters of recommendation become even more important. Even one well thought out and laudatory letter of recommendation can push you into the admit category, while a handful of lukewarm endorsements can leave you to languish on the wait list or be rejected as nobody special.

There are several strategies for ensuring that your letters of recommendation are outstanding. The first and most obvious is to approach your letter writers at the earliest possible moment. Professors and others whom you will ask to write for you are busy. You must be considerate of their other time commitments, and that means approaching them early and being patient with them. Be very clear what the deadline is, and let them know that you would appreciate it if they would send in the letter as soon as possible. Always provide neatly pre-addressed and pre-stamped envelopes for their convenience.

It is your job to prompt your letter writers to actually write and post the letters on time. Prompt them no less than once per week. Many professors try to catch up on their work during long weekends and holidays, so it is a good idea to put a little extra pressure on them right before such breaks. Be sure to let a letter writer know if his letter is the last item you need—many schools will not review your application file until it is complete, so having your essay and application in three months early is of little use if your last letter of recommendation arrives after the deadline. It is a good idea to solicit at least one more letter of recommendation than the targeted school or program requires.

You should select your letter writers carefully, using three criteria: Do they know you well enough to write about you in a detailed and persuasive manner? Will they say wonderful things about you? Are they reliable enough to write and post your recommendations in a timely manner?

Schools usually prefer that you have letters of recommendation written by employers and professors who have the most intimate knowledge of your work and study habits. A specific letter from your immediate supervisor will have more weight than a vague letter from someone higher up in the organization who obviously does not know you very well. Some letters may have two signatories, such as a full professor and a teaching assistant, or the president of the company and the vice president of sales.

Of course, you should select letter writers who will say the most wonderful things about you. Some professors are known for writing letters of recommendation that are timely, well wrought, and successful; you should ask around and discover who they are. Do not assume that just because someone is friendly with you that she will write a good letter for you. A professor or supervisor who respects you, no matter how she feels about you personally, is probably the best bet.

Finally, it is not a good idea to inadvertently fail to select someone from whom the admissions committee will be expecting a letter. If you conducted a senior research project or wrote an honors thesis, the committee will be expecting a letter from your faculty advisor. If you reported directly to the president at your last company, the committee will be expecting a letter from that president. On the other hand, you may have good reason to *intentionally* fail to solicit a letter from one of these people.

When you have your list of preferred writers, sit down with them and ask them to tell you honestly what they could say about you in a letter of recommendation. This can be tough, but it is far better to find out that a professor is not able to endorse your candidacy than it is to have your targeted school find this out before you! Sometimes you can negotiate with your professors. You might get them to agree not to mention your habit of turning in papers late, and to keep the focus of the letter on the quality of your writing and scholarship, for example. If you feel that someone is less than thrilled to write a letter of recommendation for you, select someone else. A reluctant and tepid "endorsement" can be the kiss of death.

If your letter writer is an articulate, skilled writer who thinks you can walk on water, do not prep him or put words into his mouth. You will find that he can craft a far better letter than you could imagine. If your letter writer is *not* all of the above, then it is perfectly acceptable to provide a list of salient points you think might be appropriate to address in the letter. To jog your author's memory, you can also provide him with a sample of your best paper, your curriculum vitae or résumé, a list of your college activities, or some other evidence of outstanding performance. This is especially apt if you have not worked directly with this person for some time.

If your school provides a letter forwarding service, then your professors will write fairly vague "To Whom It May Concern" letters for your file, which are then forwarded to the schools and programs you specify. Although there is a great deal of mystique about the confidentiality of letters of recommendation, you can check the letters in your file rather easily. If you have a friend in graduate school or a friend who is a college instructor, have your file forwarded to that friend. You need not fabricate a pretense, just request that your file be sent to "Attn: Your Friend, Graduate School of Whatever, Major University, USA." Many letter forwarding services will also forward your file to potential employers. If you question the ethics of this, I would like to remind you that professors can be arbitrary, careless, and even spiteful. Be sure to read the exact terms of your confidentiality contract and abide by the letter of the agreement. (In most cases, for example, it would be unethical for your friend to forward copies of the actual letters to you.) Letters of recommendation are so critical a part of the graduate admissions process that you need to be sure that yours are laudatory. If you discover that one is not, *you must have it removed from your file.*

Even if your school uses a letter forwarding service, it is a good idea to beseech your professors to craft personal letters for each school you approach. You may be applying to medical school and a doctoral program in anthropology at the same time, and the same letter of recommendation for both targets will not serve your best interests.

Be sure to send prompt and sincere thank-you notes to all your letter authors. One doctoral student wrote, "You'll find that you use them again and again, and they'll be more inclined to help you next time if you really appreciate it this time." Students sometimes view graduate school as an end goal, but it is actually just one more step in the continuing process of joining academia or launching a professional career.

If a professor is particularly enthusiastic about you, have her call up your targeted school and intercede on your behalf. This will be most effective if she knows someone where you are going, which is frequently the case. (You should note that this is how most academic *jobs* are obtained, as well, so practice getting these extra endorsements now.)

In the event that a professor or employer asks you to provide a first draft of your letter of recommendation, *do not hold back.* This is no time to be shy or humble; rather, it is a time to take advantage of a golden opportunity. When writing such a letter, pretend that you are the person who is going to sign the letter. Then, think of yourself as a singularly outstanding candidate for the graduate program you have selected. Remember, if the signatory does not like something you have written, she can ask you to change it.

Here are some of the components of an effective letter of recommendation: The author demonstrates her credentials for writing such a letter. How well does this writer know the candidate? How qualified is this writer to objectively evaluate the candidate's past performance and future potential? What particular expertise does the writer have that would be impressive testimony to her ability to judge? The best letters are almost personal in answering these questions. Here is an opening paragraph that exemplifies this approach:

> When I first met Katrina Katzienko nine years ago, she had just emigrated with her family from the Soviet Union. She did not speak a word of English, and my daughter was her tutor for one year. I watched as she mastered this language, and she ended up tutoring my daughter

in algebra. Much later, she enrolled at [major university], where she has been a star student in theoretical physics. As chairman of the department, I selected her as my research assistant, the first undergraduate to have this post since I took over the department twenty-two years ago . . .

An effective letter will address the candidate's intellectual capacity, work habits, social skills, and particular academic preparation. These statements need a frame of reference, so some letter authors will rank students in a greater context, such as "I find Ms. Ashton's academic performance to fall consistently in the top 10 percent of students I have ever instructed," or "Mr. Herzel is a solid student, certainly ranking in the top half of students at St. Johns, but you have to take this ranking in the context that the overwhelming majority of St. Johns' students obtain an advanced degree within ten years of graduation, most of them from the top programs in the nation."

Some letters will describe specific academic accomplishments that illustrate the student's abilities. Such letters are usually compelling because the reader can judge for herself the performance described. (This is also a particularly apt style of letter to request if you have a spotty career. Ask your professor or employer to focus the entire letter on your most successful project.)

Authors often cite challenges the student has overcome, or unusual aspects of the student's background. In order to remain believable and to demonstrate objectivity, letters of recommendation almost always contain some modicum of criticism or warn of some weakness. So, if you review your own letters and discover moderate criticism, do not despair. In an outstanding letter, of course, the weakness will be a strength in disguise, just as in the essays; for example: "If Johanna has any fault it is that she spends too much time on her extracurricular activities. However, as you can see her academic performance remains excellent."

One admissions reader told me that he is particularly impressed when a professor cites a student's contributions to her undergraduate department or school. On a similar note, one highly successful candidate told me, "The trick is to look like a rising star, somebody who is going on to do wonderful things whether you attend their school or not. Remember, in the long run *they* want to be associated with *you*." Graduate schools are seeking people who will contribute to their programs as outstanding students, who will enhance the reputation of the program by the success of their careers, and who will later on return to be involved as benefactors. A good letter of recommendation will definitely predict a bright future for the candidate, as a scholar and as a professional with a career. This is often an effective way to close a letter of recommendation.

As you read the sample letters of recommendation in this chapter, look for these components: credentials of the writer; depth of knowledge of the candidate as a person and as a performer; testimony as to the candidate's intellectual capacity, work habits, and preparedness for graduate studies; some small fault to demonstrate the writer's objectivity; and predictions of the candidate's future career contributions.

LETTER OF RECOMMENDATION #1

Note how this first letter covers all the bases, touching on the candidate's analytical skills, interpersonal aptitude, and mental acuity in general. The letter was from the president of a finance company, and was on company stationery, of course. The details of the candidate's career are covered in other submissions, especially his résumé and his application essay, so this letter is free to focus on the president's impressions of the candidate.

Letter from the President of the Company for Graduate School of Business

¶1   I am pleased to write this letter of recommendation for Shane Whittington to attend graduate school in business. I have close daily experience of Shane's work habits and contributions to this company, and I can only report that I rank him in the top 5% of business people I have ever had the pleasure to know.

¶2   His analytical abilities are first rate. In addition to his research and reporting work, he has designed several methodologies that are now in use throughout the company. Even more important, and perhaps harder to define, he always understands the reasoning or the goal behind any analysis that he performs. This is a rare and refreshing trait.

¶3   His interpersonal skills are one of his most outstanding traits. Everybody who knows him thinks favorably of him, and I know I can trust him to represent the company to our numerous shareholders and business associates. He is enthusiastic and optimistic in his dealings with investors, and this has been of benefit to the company. Shane's duties have included several opportunities for direct sales, and it is clear that he could have a highly successful career in this area should he choose to do so.

¶4   In short, when I give an assignment to Shane I know it will be done right, on time, and in excess of my specifications. If he has any fault, it is adding enhancements to assignments, doing more than what was asked. In summary, he is a tremendous asset to management, and will surely rise rapidly in any organization in which he is employed.

LETTER OF RECOMMENDATION #2

The next letter is short, sweet, and overwhelmingly effective. I read three letters recommending this student, and each was unequivocal and unreserved in its praise. This student does not appear to have any faults, so none is mentioned! Note how the author describes the candidate's performance in a specific class so clearly that the reader is able to think to herself, "I want a special student like that."

Letter from Professor for Graduate School of English

¶1   It is a great pleasure for me to recommend Ms. Celeste Wallace for admission, and fellowship support, to graduate school in English. I first encountered her in a large lecture course I was teaching three years ago. Within days, Ms. Wallace had distinguished herself as an absolutely extraordinary student—one who could ask the most penetrating questions about the assigned reading and to expound her ideas with effortless extemporaneous elegance. I soon found that in a class of 150 students, I was beginning to carry on a dialogue with just one— much to the fascination of her classmates, who seemed as awestruck as I was. Not surprisingly, Celeste's written work proved to be of the same caliber as her conversation; she received a grade of A+, and even that seemed inadequate to her accomplishment.

¶2   Since then, I have stayed in touch with Ms. Wallace and have helped to steer her toward courses worthy of her gifts. I have read four of her subsequently written papers, and have noted in them a deepening and broadening of theoretical concerns. With her boundless curiosity and energy, her wit, her good humor, and her blazing intelligence, she has all the makings of a first-rate critic and college teacher. I would rank her among the top few undergraduates I have ever taught in thirty-three years at Michigan.

LETTER OF RECOMMENDATION #3

Schools also occasionally solicit letters from peers. Professors and employers are trained professionals, practiced in the arts of innuendo and scratch-my-back-I'll-scratch-yours. Peers can be guileless, which is exactly why schools request these letters. (Peers often convey more unintentionally than intentionally. The first thing a candidate reveals about himself is the quality of his friends and his judgment, so pick authors of peer letters very carefully.) The letter presented here is nearly perfect. It gives a strong picture of the candidate's capacities and stamina, and the degrees listed at the bottom are a nice touch, establishing the credentials of the author. One does wish one had a greater feel for the personality of the person described, however. This letter is presented in full so you can see the proper layout for such a letter.

Peer Letter for Medical School

Geoffrey Savage
196 Foulswell Street, #1-B
Boston, Massachusetts 02125
(617) 555-3063

Office of Admissions and Student Affairs
University of Minnesota Medical School
Box 293 UMHC
420 Delaware Street SE
Minneapolis, Minnesota 55455-0310

September 8, 1991

Attn: Selection Committee
Contents: Letter of Evaluation from Roommate for
            Applicant Robert Savage, SS# 681-15-0339

Dear Committee:

¶1   Robert Savage has been my roommate for the last four years—he is also my brother. I am proud to have Robert as a brother. He is a person of strong ideals, he is a serious person, and he is someone on whom his friends can count. We are roommates by choice and friendship, not just because we are brothers.

¶2   As to Robert's qualifications for medical school, I know of his strong aptitude, especially in the sciences, his long intent to go to medical school, and his daily work habits.

¶3 If I were to pick a few words to describe my brother, at least from my point of view as his roommate, it would be: busy, active, efficient. Robert is someone who is always doing something. He takes on more than most people, and I have watched him effortlessly handle a very large load of commitments (classes, sports, clubs, and social activities) that would make other students fall apart.

¶4 One of the reasons Robert is able to do so much is because of his study habits. He studies every evening for one to five hours except when he has a class or lab. He plans for his tests and presentations so that he doesn't have a work "crunch" in the last few days. In addition to this, he seems to get any science subject on the first pass through. I have learned a lot from him about good study habits, mostly about planning ahead, but I know few students who "get" the material so easily. In his lab groups, many sessions of which have met here in our apartment, he is usually the natural leader, setting the strategy for the lab and the write up.

¶5 Robert is a good roommate because he never complains about anything. I enjoy his company, and we have many friends together. We are both pretty busy, actually, so it is good that we enjoy the company of each other.

¶6 Robert has many strengths—strong intellect, a level-headed personality, he knows a lot of people all over campus—but if he has any weakness it is forgetting to take the time to relax more and "smell the roses." I think his ability to focus his attentions on a goal and ignore all distractions is probably handy for medical school, though.

¶7 I recommend Robert Savage for acceptance to your medical program. I know that he will be able to excel in your program, and I know that he will be a highly professional, skilled, and compassionate physician. Besides, you should know that his nickname already is "Doc" Savage.

¶8 Thank you for this opportunity to speak up on Robert's behalf.

Sincerely yours,

Geoffrey Savage

B.A., History (History of Navigation Systems), Boston University, May 1990

Ph.D. candidate, History of Science, M.I.T., currently

LETTER OF RECOMMENDATION #4

The next letter is for a postdoctoral residency in orthodontics. The salutation was "To Whom It May Concern," as the candidate applied to a number of programs. Nevertheless, the letter is warm and personal, and clearly demonstrates how a student's contributions to his own school enhance his desirability as a graduate or postgraduate candidate. It is clear that this candidate provided the author of the letter with a complete list of his accomplishments and activities.

Letter from Dean of School of Dentistry for Residency in Orthodontics

¶1   It is my pleasure to write a letter of recommendation on behalf of Akira Tokuyoshi in his pursuit of postdoctoral education in the field of orthodontics. I can state unequivocally that his academic and clinical skills have placed him among the top students in his class. His polite manner, his concern for his studies and his patients, and his emotional maturity are well known and respected among his peers and the faculty and staff.

¶2   His academic credentials alone qualify him for post-doctoral study and advanced training, but I can recommend this student enthusiastically for other reasons as well. He has complemented his academic schedule with leadership activities in many extracurricular areas, and has enhanced the reputation and the image of [major university] Dental School as much as a student can.

¶3   Akira was selected student editor of the [major university] Dental School's journal, *The Dental Explorer*. As such, he has worked closely with many faculty and students to put together the 1991 issue, which will be released soon, and which has already been highly praised by the faculty reviewers.

¶4   Akira has served (by invitation) as a preceptor in the [major university] Dental School's Summer Enrichment Program. There he taught dental morphology and head and neck anatomy to incoming dental students. Also, he has volunteered as a tutor for the preclinical laboratory classes every year since his arrival. In these capacities, his professors have rated him very highly on both communication skills and technical knowledge. His concern for this fellow students is admirable, and a credit to himself and the success of our program.

¶5 Akira's natural ability to work with and motivate others has helped him hold several offices. He is currently president of our campus chapter of Delta Sigma Delta, the international dental fraternity, and he is vice president and senior editor of our Student Research Group, an IADR affiliate to promote primary research in dental science.

¶6 Akira has also participated in research with distinguished members of our faculty, and has participated in several presentations and table clinics at scientific meetings. I understand that somehow he finds time to play sports as well.

¶7 In summary, Akira distinguishes himself as an individual who exhibits an organized, scientific approach to work, an ability to plan, organize, and implement projects of varying complexity. He is a team player, who with a high degree of motivation, innovation and initiative, can accomplish his goals.

¶8 I know him to be a most personable and sincere young man, well liked and respected by those who work with him. I enthusiastically recommend this individual as an outstanding future orthodontist, and I predict he will have a bright future.

LETTER OF RECOMMENDATION #5

Fellowships and scholarships often require letters of recommendation in addition to an essay and an application. The following is a classic letter of recommendation, citing the author's intimate knowledge of the candidate's background, then praising her strengths in all areas necessary for success in the field in question. In addition, the author is a well known figure to the members of the fellowship awards committee. The letter is to the Urban Land Institute (ULI), Land Use and Development Fellowships Awards Committee, and the salutation is "To the Awards Committee." I would like to point out that letters like this, combined with a persuasive application and a cogent essay, are worth thousands of dollars.

Letter from Former Employer for Fellowship Award

¶1   I worked with Maureen Daly, an applicant for the ULI Land Use and Development Fellowship, for five years while she was employed by the East Bay Regional Park District. As a program analyst in the Land Acquisition Department, she was invaluable in a wide variety of acquisition and land planning projects. The issues that Maureen dealt with were involved, sensitive, and difficult. She proved time and again that she was capable of handling complex land use and development issues, often in the face of opposition. Many acquisitions involved developers, planners from several local governments, and a variety of community groups; she worked well with each. She was always well informed, prepared, and insightful on the range of interests represented.

¶2   I consider among Maureen's strengths her genuine enthusiasm for the subject of land use planning and development, her ability to analyze the subject at hand and cut through the mire to the essence of the situation, her attention to the necessary details (including numbers), and her intelligence. She was an outstanding employee.

¶3   Maureen Daly is an excellent choice for this fellowship; she has my highest recommendation.

LETTER OF RECOMMENDATION #6

Although professors and employers are first-choice authors of letters of recommendation, sometimes someone else with a long-term personal knowledge of you can be quite persuasive. The next two letters are "character witness" letters. Admissions committees are not impressed if *all* your letters of recommendation are of this type; they are most effective when submitted in addition to a full set of letters from individuals with an intimate knowledge of your work and study capacities. If your character witness cannot add compelling weight to your application, it may be a good idea to forgo such a letter altogether. Note how the following letter is full of factual evidence for the committee's consideration.

Letter from Rabbi

¶1   I am pleased to recommend to you Aaron [last name withheld]. It is my opinion that Aaron will make an uncommonly good medical doctor, and that he has demonstrated character traits which will ensure this. Since I have known him well over ten years, I hope my letter will have weight of consideration commensurate with that length of time.

¶2   My organization, International Organization for Sepharadic Rescue (I.O.S.R.), is dedicated to rescuing Sepharadic Jews from oppressive regimes, mostly in the Middle East. We brought Aaron [last name withheld] to New York City from Iran ten years ago, after the fall of the Shah. He was a child of eleven years when he emigrated from Iran, leaving his parents behind. It was thought at the time that they would complete some business matters and follow their son, but in fact they were detained for several years.

¶3   During this time, from when he was eleven until he was thirteen, Aaron lived under the benevolent protection of I.O.S.R. He lived in a dormitory situation, and in the homes of several of some of our more dedicated members. He was always a delight to us all, and his personal strength and courage were a testament to human potential. I say this not out of appreciation for his ability to carry on without his own parents, and in spite of his deep and ongoing concern for them, but because of his ability to *excel* and *thrive* in these adverse conditions.

¶4   Being of a young age, he mastered the English language and went on to study at the Talmudical Seminary here in New York, a very rigorous Orthodox Jewish high school with a national reputation. There he excelled in a program of science, religion and classical liberal arts (just for the record, all subjects except Hebrew language studies are taught in English). He was the valedictorian of his class, and he of course graduated with honors.

¶5   Then at just the moment when some students would have gone on to a carefree college experience, Aaron's parents finally arrived from Iran. I know of his dedication and his daily assistance to them. He smoothed the path for these new immigrants who were without the language and social skills he had learned so well. At the same time, he was highly active in youth programs for I.O.S.R., rising to the position of Director of Youth Programs, including our summer program involving hundreds of students.

¶6   So you see how I have watched this young man grow and develop, and I know the tremendous focus he has upon his studies and his service to mankind. It is my firm belief that his maturity, initiative, and self-reliance could only lead to success in medical school, and that his strength of character could only lead to an outstanding contribution to humanity as a medical doctor.

¶7   I highly recommend Aaron to your school. It is my unconditional belief that he will become an ethical, compassionate and extremely competent physician.

LETTER OF RECOMMENDATION #7

The next example demonstrates a different kind of character witness letter. The author is someone who is very well known, and who by his long association with the candidate and his family, is able to give a new perspective on the candidate's application. Again, a letter such as this will only be effective if the rest of the application and the other letters of recommendation corroborate it. This sort of letter is risky, as members of the admissions committee could be offended if they interpret the letter as "coattail riding." This letter, however, works, mostly due to the fact that the author seems to have relatively close knowledge of the candidate and a genuine affection for him.

Letter from Prominent Friend of the Family

¶1   It is with great pleasure that I write this letter of recommendation for Mr. Whitney Arden to enter the medical program at _____.

¶2   I have known Whitney and his family for many years, and I can vouch for his intellectual acuity, his maturity, and his zest for life. He is an unusual young man, displaying a goal-oriented approach to life and a sense of responsibility and purpose far beyond his years. In a conversation I had with him many years ago, he was quite articulate about his desire to be a doctor. I am pleased to see his resolute attachment to that ideal.

¶3   As you may well know, there are many things Whitney could do. He has the resources to pursue any calling, and for this reason his determination to pursue a life of service in medicine is all the more admirable. I am sure you are aware of his desire to serve in a clinic in a Third World country.

¶4   I know Whitney's parents well. I have witnessed his family's support of his educational goals, and at the same time, I can report that the particular nature of his calling is entirely his own. Although he could have studied anywhere in Europe, at his initiative he came back to the United States from Austria to study pre-medicine. Whitney has lived on his own since he was 16 or 17, to the best of my knowledge. His relationship with his family is close, yet he is quite an independent man.

¶5   Incidentally, Whitney has always been a friendly, articulate young man with many friends. His social skills belie his many hours in the laboratory. He has spent some holidays at my home in Los Angeles and I have traveled with him and his parents. He is a perfect guest and gentleman, always charming and seemingly able to get along with anyone.

¶6   I know that Whitney Arden would make a solid contribution to the ranks of your alumni some day. His views of responsible citizenship and, although he would never use the term, noblesse oblige make him a student from which we can all expect a future of 'good works.'

¶7   I recommend him due to his integrity, his intelligence, and his admirable goals in life. I predict that he will pursue and excel at a career in public service.

■ BIBLIOGRAPHY ■

The resources listed here are some of the books available to you, but only some. New titles and new editions of existing titles are released almost every month. Use this bibliography as a place to launch your research, and take particular note of the guides that lead you to other guides.

Writing Aids

A writer's best friend is still the ordinary dictionary. Any student without a recent edition of a good dictionary on her desk should not breathe before she has rectified this deficiency. Some of the guides listed below are meant to be read before writing, such as *On Writing Well* and *The Elements of Style,* and others are meant to be used as a reference, to look up matters of style as you come to them, such as *The Chicago Manual of Style.*

Webster's Ninth New Collegiate Dictionary. Springfield, MA: Merriam-Webster, Inc., 1989.

Roget's Thesaurus of English Words and Phrases by Susan M. Lloyd. White Plains, NY: Longman, 1989.

On Writing Well: An Informal Guide to Writing Nonfiction by William Zinsser. New York: Harper and Row, 4th ed. 1990.

The Elements of Style by William Strunk and E. B. White. New York: Macmillan, 3rd ed. 1979.

Edit Yourself: A Manual for Everyone Who Works with Words by Bruce Ross-Larson. New York: Norton, 1982.

Miss Thistlebottom's Hobgoblins by Theodore M. Bernstein. New York: Simon & Schuster, 1984.

Nonsexist Word Finder: A Dictionary of Gender-Free Usage by Rosalie Maggio. Phoenix, AZ: Oryx Press, 1987.

Nonsexist Communicator: Solving the Problems of Gender and Awkwardness in Modern English by Bobbye Sorrels. Englewood Cliffs, NJ: Prentice Hall, 1983.

Fowler's English Dictionary by Henry Fowler. New York: Smith Pubs., 1989.

The Chicago Manual of Style. Chicago: University of Chicago Press, 13th ed., 1982.

The Associated Press Stylebook by E. Powell and H. Agione. New York: Dell, 1990.

Guides That Tell You Where to Go

Some of the guides under this heading were listed in Chapter 1, *Choosing a School or Program;* the rest are a sampling of the more esoteric guides available to discovering programs in your area of interest. In more specialized areas, very good programs may be tucked away in otherwise undistinguished schools, and mediocre programs may lurk in rather renowned institutions. This is hardly an exhaustive listing, but it should give you an idea of the type of guides available for those interested in every field from ichthyology to deconstructionism.

Accounting to Zoology: Graduate Fields Defined. ed. by Amy J. Goldstein. Princeton, NJ: Peterson's, 1987.

Peterson's Guide to Graduate and Professional Programs: An Overview. Princeton, NJ: Peterson's, 1991.

Directory of Graduate Programs: 1990-1991, 4 vols. Princeton, NJ: Educational Testing Service, 1989.

Peterson's Guide to Graduate Programs in Business, Education, Health, and Law. Princeton, NJ: Peterson's, 1991.

Peterson's Guide to Graduate Programs in the Humanities and Social Sciences. Princeton, NJ: Peterson's, 1991.

Peterson's Guide to Graduate Programs in the Physical Sciences and Mathematics. Princeton, NJ: Peterson's, 1991.

Peterson's Guide to Graduate Programs in the Biological and Agricultural Sciences. Princeton, NJ: Peterson's, 1991.

Peterson's Guide to Graduate Programs in Engineering and Applied Sciences, Princeton, NJ: Peterson's, 1991.

Assessment of Research-Doctorate Programs in the United States, ed. by Lyle V. Jones, et al. Washington DC: National Academy Press, 1982.

The Insider's Guide to the Top Fifteen Law Schools by Cynthia L. Cooper. New York: Doubleday, 1990.

Looking at Law School: A Student Guide from the Society of American Law School Teachers, ed. by Stephen Gillers. New York: NAL, 1990.

The Official Guide to U.S. Law Schools 1989-89: Prelaw Handbook, ed. by Thomas O. White and Bruce I. Zimmer. Newtown, PA: Law School Admission Services, 1988.

Barron's Guide to Medical and Dental Schools by Saul Wischnitzer. Hanppange, NY: Barron's Educational Series, 4th ed., 1989.

Directory of Graduate Medical Education Programs 1990-1991. Chicago: American Medical Association, 1990.

Allied Health Education Directory, ed. by Gloria C. Gupta, et al. Chicago: American Medical Association, 18th ed., 1990.

Business Week's Guide to the Best Business Schools, John A. Byrne, et al. New York: McGraw-Hill, 1989.

Barron's Guide to Graduate Business Schools by Eugene Miller. Hauppauge, NY: Barron's Educational Series, 7th ed. 1990.

Insider's Guide to the Top Ten Business Schools, ed. by Tom Fischgrund. Boston: Little, Brown & Co, 1988.

Directory of Graduate Research. Washington, DC: American Chemical Society, 1977.

Graduate Programs in Chemistry. Washington, DC: American Chemical Society, 1983.

The American Film Institute Guide to Film and Television Courses. New York: Arco, 8th ed., 1990.

Dance Directory: Programs of Professional Preparation in American Colleges and Universities, ed. by Vera Lundahl. Reston VA: National Dance Association, 1986.

Directory of Professional Preparation Programs in TESOL in the United States, 1989-1991 by Julia Frank-McNeil with C.R. Byrne. Washington DC: Teachers of English to Speakers of Other Languages, 1989.

Directory of Women's Studies Programs and Library Resources, ed. by Beth Stafford. Phoenix, AZ: Oryx Press, 1990.

Graduate Programs in Physics, Astronomy and Related Fields, 1984-1985, ed. by Dion Shea. New York: American Institute of Physics, 1984.

Graduate Study in Psychology and Associated Fields, 1988 Edition with 1989 Addendum. Washington DC: American Psychological Association, 1989.

Guide to American Art Schools by John D. Werenko. New York: Penguin, 1988.

Guide to Departments of Geography in the United States and Canada, ed. by Sally Meyers. Washington, DC: Association of American Geographers, 1989.

Guide to Graduate Education in Speech-Language Pathology and Audiology, 1988-1989. Rockville, MD: American Speech-Language Hearing Association, 1988.

Guide to Graduate Study in Economics, Agricultural Economics, and Doctoral Programs in Business and Administration in the United States and Canada, ed. by W. Owen and D. Ruby. Boulder, CO: Economics Institute, 8th ed., 1989.

Guide to Schools and Departments of Religion and Seminaries in the United States and Canada, compiled by Modoc Press Inc. Staff. New York: MacMillan, 1986.

Japanese Studies in the United States, Part II: Directory of Japan Specialists and Japanese Studies Institutions in the United States and Canada, ed. by Patricia G. Steinhoff. Ann Arbor, MI: Association for Asian Studies, 1989.

Register of Environmental Engineering Graduate Programs by G. Amy and W. Knocke. Austin, TX: Association of Environmental Engineering Professors, 6th ed., 1989.

The Schirmer Guide to Schools of Music and Conservatories throughout the World by Nancy Uscher. New York: Schirmer Books, 1988.

Bricker's International Directory, Volume I: Long-Term University-Based Executive Programs. Princeton, NJ: Peterson's, 1991.

Bricker's International Directory, Volume II: Short-Term University-Based Executive Programs. Princeton, NJ: Peterson's, 1991.

The Encyclopedia of Associations, Volume I: National Organizations, ed. by Karin E. Koek, et al. Detroit: Gale Research, Inc., 1989. Note: Associations serving your future profession often publish lists of recommended graduate programs, and can give you other information on such valuable topics as accreditation. Call or write and ask.

Guides That Tell You How to Pay for It

Virtually every student should make a full financial, fellowship, and scholarship application along with her application for admission. The following guides will help you get ideas on sources for monies and grants, but the best approach remains to work very closely with the graduate program to which you are applying. Remember, you can often play programs off against one another to get the aid package you want from the school you want. Once again, these listings are meant to be representative, not exhaustive.

The Graduate Scholarship Book by Daniel J. Cassidy. Englewood Cliffs, NJ: Prentice Hall, 1988).

How to Find Out about Financial Aid: A Guide to over 700 Directories Listing Scholarships, Fellowships, Grants, Loans, Awards, and Internships by Gail Ann Schlachter. San Carlos, CA: Reference Service Press, 1987.

Financial Aids for Higher Education by Oreon Keeslar. Dubuque, IA: William C. Brown, 14th ed., 1991.

Peterson's Grants for Graduate Students. Princeton, NJ: Peterson's Guides, 3rd ed., 1991.

Directory of Financial Aids for Minorities, 1989-1990 by Gail Ann Schlachter. Los Angeles, CA: Reference Service Press, 1989.

Directory of Financial Aids for Women, 1989-1990 by Gail Ann Schlachter. Los Angeles, CA: References Service Press, 1989.

Barron's Guide to Financing a Medical School Education by Marguerite J. Dennis. Hauppauge, NY: Barron's Educational Series, 1990.

Free Money for Humanities and Social Sciences by Laurie Blum. New York: Paragon House, 1987.

Free Money for Mathematical and Natural Sciences by Laurie Blum. New York: Paragon House, 1987.

Free Money for Professional Studies by Laurie Blum. New York: Paragon House, 1987.

Corporate Tuition Aid Programs by Joseph P. O'Neill. Princeton, NJ: Peterson's, 1986.

Financial Resources for International Study, compiled by The Institute of International Education. Princeton, NJ: Peterson's, 1989.

Financing Your Law School Education by Tom Voss and Marianne Fiorentine. Newtown, PA: Law School Admission Services, 1987.

Study Guides and Other Publications
Related to Graduate Admissions Exams

Some students reported that they were well prepared for and comfortable with their graduate examinations, and thought formal classroom exam preparation was a waste of money; others reported that the in-class training was invaluable for test-taking strategies alone. Since taking these prep classes can cost hundreds of dollars, whether to take formal prep classes is not a frivolous decision. In every case, however, students should buy and study *more than one* exam preparation booklet such as the ones listed here.

Graduate Record Examination (GRE)
    ETS
    P.O. Box 6000
    Princeton, NJ 08541-6000
    Phone: 609-771-7670

GRE Information Bulletin (free)

Practicing to Take the GRE General Test

Practicing to Take the GRE {Subject Test Name Here} Test

Graduate Management Admissions Test (GMAT)
    ETS
    P.O. Box 6103
    Princeton, NJ 08541-6103
    phone: 609-771-7330

GMAT Bulletin of Information (free)

The Official Guide for GMAT Review

The Official Software for GMAT Review

Law School Admission Test (LSAT)
    Law School Admissions Service
    Box 2000
    Newtown, PA 18940-0998
    phone: 215-968-1100

Law Services Information Book (free)

Medical College Admission Test (MCAT)
    Association of American Medical Colleges
    Attn: Membership and Publication Orders
    One Dupont Circle, NW, Suite 200
    Washington, DC 20036
    phone: 202-828-0416

MCAT Student Manual

Medical School Admissions Requirements

Total Math Review for the GMAT, GRE, and Other Graduate School Admission Tests by David Frieder. New York: Arco, 1981.

Barron's How to Prepare for the GRE: Graduate Record Examination, General Test by Samuel C. Brownstein, et al. Hauppauge, NY: Barron's Educational Series, 9th ed., 1990.

Graduate Record Examination General Test (GRE) by T. Martinson and G. Crocett. New York: Arco, 2nd ed., 1987.

LSAT: Law School Admission Test by T.H. Martinson. Englewood Cliffs, NJ: Prentice Hall, 3rd. ed., 1989.

Complete Preparation for the MCAT by J. L. Flowers et al. Bethesda, MD: Betz Publishing, 1988.

Barron's How to Prepare for the Graduate Record Examination—GRE: Biology Test by J. Snyder and C. Rodgers. Hauppauge, NY: Barron's Educational Series, 1989.

GRE Biology Test Preparation. West Piscataway, NJ: Research and Education Association, 1988.

GRE Chemistry Test Preparation. West Piscataway, NJ: Research and Education Association, 1988.

GRE Mathematics Test Preparation. West Piscataway, NJ: Research and Education Association, 1989.

Barron's How to Prepare for the Graduate Record Examination—GRE: The Psychology Test by Edward L. Palmer. Hauppauge, NY: Barron's Educational Series, 1989.

Interview Books

None of these books is specifically aimed at graduate applications interviewing, however, all three contain great information that will help you prepare for an interview, avoid gaffes, and shine in your presentation.

Sweaty Palms by M. Anthony Medley. Berkeley, CA: Ten Speed Press, 2nd. ed., 1991.

Hot Tips, Sneaky Tricks, and Last-Ditch Tactics: An Insider's Guide to Getting your First Corporate Job by Jeff Speck. New York: John Wiley and Sons, 1989.

Knock 'em Dead: With Great Answers to Tough Interview Questions by Martin J. Yate. Holbrook, MA: Adams, Bob, Inc., 4th ed., 1989.

Miscellaneous Recommended Reading

Full Disclosure: Do You Really Want to Be a Lawyer by Susan J. Bell. Princeton, NJ: Peterson's, 1989.

Running from the Law: Why Good Lawyers Are Getting Out of the Legal Profession by Deborah L. Arron. Berkeley, CA: Ten Speed Press, 1991.

Medical School Admissions: The Insider's Guide by J. Zebala and D. Jones. Memphis, TN: Mustang Publishing Company, 1989.

The Overnight Résumé by D. Asher. Berkeley, CA: Ten Speed Press, 1991.

What to Do if You Don't Get In

You can always join the French Foreign Legion. For more information, write to:

Bureau de la Legionne Étranger
Quartier Vienot
13400 Aubagne
FRANCE

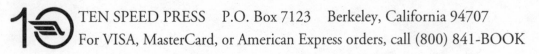